Dedication.

This book is dedicated to the Christian in the spiritual trenches. Who's taking the battle to the enemy. Who refuses to be defeated. Who hopes against hope.

I Talk Back to
the Devil

by Doug Giles

Copyright 2024, Doug Giles, All Rights Reserved
No part of this book may be reproduced, stored in a retrieval system, or transmitted by any means without the written permission of the author.

Published by White Feather Press. (www.whitefeatherpress.com)
Edited by Karen Walker.
ISBN 978-1-61808-218-3
Printed in the United States of America
Cover design by David Bugnon and mobopolis.com

Scriptures marked (KJV) are taken from the KING JAMES VERSION (KJV): KING JAMES VERSION, public domain.

Scripture quotations marked (MSG) are taken from The Message, copyright © 1993, 2002, 2018 by Eugene H. Peterson. Used by permission of NavPress. All rights reserved. Represented by Tyndale House Publishers.

Scripture quotations taken from the (NASB®) New American Standard Bible®, Copyright © 1960, 1971, 1977, 1995 by The Lockman Foundation. Used by permission. All rights reserved. lockman.org

Scripture quotations marked (EASY) are taken from the Easy-English Bible Copyright © MissionAssist 2019 - Charitable Incorporated Organisation 1162807. Used by permission. All rights reserved.

Scripture quotations marked (NIV) are taken from the Holy Bible, New International Version®, NIV®. Copyright © 1973, 1978, 1984, 2011 by Biblica, Inc.™ Used by permission of Zondervan. All rights reserved worldwide. www.zondervan.comThe "NIV" and "New International Version" are trademarks registered in the United States Patent and Trademark Office by Biblica, Inc.™

Scripture quotations marked (TLB) are taken from The Living Bible, copyright © 1971 by Tyndale House Foundation. Used by permission of Tyndale House Publishers, Carol Stream, Illinois 60188. All rights reserved.

Scripture quotations marked (ESV) are from the ESV® Bible (The Holy Bible, English Standard Version®), © 2001 by Crossway, a publishing ministry of Good News Publishers. Used by permission. All rights reserved.https://www.crossway.org/permissions/

Table of Contents

Introduction.
Our Wealth In Christ.
Proclamation #1. God Will Crush My Enemies. — 1
Proclamation #2. God Will Bless Me with Holy Growth. — 7
Proclamation #3. When The Enemy Says, "You're Cursed" Shout This To Him. — 11
Proclamation #4. This Proclamation Will Light Wet Wood. — 17
Proclamation #5. When Buried Under A Mountain of Sin, God'll Show Me Grace. — 23
Proclamation #6. God Will Float My Financial Boat. — 29
Proclamation #7. The Name of The Lord Is A Strong Tower - Declare It! — 35
Proclamation #8. I Am A Friend of God. — 43
Proclamation #9. Your Identity in Christ. — 51
Proclamation #10. Psalm 112 - God's Blessings Upon Your Kids — 57
Our Walk in Christ.
Proclamation #11. I'm Dead to My Flesh and Alive to God. — 63
Proclamation #12. Blessed Are You When People Insult You. — 69
Proclamation #13. God Hates This Type of Person - Don't Be Like Them. — 75
Proclamation #14. Speak The Word of God with Boldness. — 81
Proclamation #15. Create In Me A Clean Heart. — 87
Proclamation #16. Walking in the Fear of the Lord. — 95
Proclamation #17. I Will Have A Godly Marriage. — 103

Proclamation #18. I Will Imitate God.	109
Proclamation #19. Make Me An Acts 2:42 Christian, Lord!	115
Proclamation #20. I Will Be A Generous and Cheerful Giver.	121
Our Warfare in Christ.	
Proclamation #21. I Will Not Live in Fear.	125
Proclamation #22. Jesus Rules and Satan Drools.	129
Proclamation #23. Adios, Evil Leaders.	135
Proclamation #24. God Dooms the Great Men of the World.	141
Proclamation #25. We Are More Than Conquerors.	147
Proclamation #26. Old and Dangerous.	153
Proclamation #27. Peace in the Storm.	161
Proclamation #28. All Authority Belongs to Jesus.	167
Proclamation #29. Speak to Your Mountain.	175
Proclamation #30. The Lord's Prayer.	179
About the Author	184
Art by Doug Giles	186
Books by Doug Giles	187

Introduction.

"What did Jesus do when he was tempted? He threw The Book at the Devil. It is written. It is written. It is written."

— Leonard Ravenhill

Dear Christian: What you have in your hands, my fellow combatant, is spiritual dynamite to demonic strongholds that seek to derail God's eternal purpose for this planet which includes you fulfilling his high calling for your life.

This book's goal is simple: my sole focus is to supply you with the biblical fodder to believe and speak when Satan tries to thwart God's kingdom expansion in your life and in his church.

Here's an FYI: What we think and say, especially when we're in the midst of a raging storm, is *muy importante*. If you think I'm full of baloney, read Numbers 13.

Numbers 13 says succinctly, if you think you're done -- you're done.

If you think you're gonna pull out of whatever garbage you're currently mired in, there's a 99.9% chance that soon you'll be footloose and fancy-free from life's quicksand. Or as Jesus put it in Matt.17:20 ...

> "The simple truth is that if you had a mere kernel of faith, a poppy seed, say, you would tell this mountain, 'Move!' and it would move. There is nothing you wouldn't be able to tackle." (MSG)

Please note that Jesus said for your mountain to move you have to speak to it. Which means you gotta get rowdy with your yapper. Talk biblical, Holy Ghost trash to your mountains, obstacles, and whatever devils are attempting to best you.

Get loud declaring God's Word over your sad situation.

Everything smells, so attitude sells.

Confess God's promises over your life with passion, faith, authority, and yes, once again, attitude.

The tongue is powerful.

According to James, an unbridled tongue can unleash hell in your life.

Check it out ...

> "Even so the tongue is a little member, and boasteth great things. Behold, how great a matter a little fire kindleth! And the tongue is a fire, a world of iniquity: so is the tongue among our members, that it defileth the whole body, and setteth on fire the course of nature; and it is set on fire of hell."
>
> – James 3:5-6 (KJV)

And according to Jesus, you can overcome Satan by Christ's shed blood, not being afraid of death, and ... via the word of your testimony. Yes, Christian, what you say has massive weight tied to it for good or for evil in your life. Behold, I give you another great example:

> "And there was war in heaven: Michael and his angels fought against the dragon; and the dragon fought and his angels, And prevailed not; neither was their place found any more in heaven. And the great dragon was cast out, that old serpent, called the Devil, and Satan, which deceiveth the whole world: he was cast out into the earth,

and his angels were cast out with him. And I heard a loud voice saying in heaven, Now is come salvation, and strength, and the kingdom of our God, and the power of his Christ: for the accuser of our brethren is cast down, which accused them before our God day and night. And they overcame him by the blood of the Lamb, and by the word of their testimony; and they loved not their lives unto the death. Therefore rejoice, ye heavens, and ye that dwell in them. Woe to the inhabiters of the earth and of the sea! for the devil is come down unto you, having great wrath, because he knoweth that he hath but a short time."

— Rev. 12:7-12 (KJV)

When Satan tempted Jesus in the wilderness, he did it with his words.

He didn't show Jesus some porn sketches he'd drawn.

He didn't do it with a Rolex that he dangled in front of an impoverished Christ.

He used his words to tempt Jesus with the lust of the flesh, the lust of the eyes, and the boastful pride of life.

So ... how did Jesus react when he was getting the best Beelzebub could toss at him?

Well, let's check it out ...

> "Then was Jesus led up of the Spirit into the wilderness to be tempted of the devil. And when he had fasted forty days and forty nights, he was afterward an hungred. And when the tempter came to him, he said, If thou be the Son of God, command that these stones be made bread. But he answered and said, It is written, Man shall not live by bread alone, but by every word that proceedeth out of the mouth of God. Then the devil taketh him up into the holy city, and setteth him on a pinnacle of the temple, And saith unto him, If thou be the Son of God, cast thyself down: for it is written, He shall give his angels charge concerning thee: and in their hands they shall bear thee up, lest at any time thou dash thy foot against a stone. Jesus said unto him, It is written again, Thou shalt not tempt the Lord thy God. Again, the devil taketh him up into an exceeding high mountain, and sheweth him all the kingdoms of the world, and the glory of them; And saith unto him, All these things will I give thee, if thou wilt fall down

and worship me. Then saith Jesus unto him, Get thee hence, Satan: for it is written, Thou shalt worship the Lord thy God, and him only shalt thou serve. Then the devil leaveth him, and, behold, angels came and ministered unto him."

– Matt. 4:1-11 (KJV)

Jesus countered *el Diablo*'s lies with the Word of God.

Please note ...

1. Jesus didn't quote Oprah.
2. Jesus didn't quote the Virgin Mary.
3. Jesus didn't quote a positive meme he saw on Instagram.
4. Jesus didn't quote Tony Robbins.
5. Jesus didn't quote the lyrics from Katy Perry's song, *Roar!*
6. Jesus didn't quote the Pope.
7. Jesus didn't quote the Southern Baptist Convention.

He quoted the Word of God.

Jesus fought Satan's words, which included a

scripture Satan had twisted, with the *verbum Dei,* and it worked. Shocker, eh?

Jesus spanked Lucifer with epic scriptural counterpunches and the Slithering One left black-eyed with his tail between his legs.

Indeed, Jesus talked back to the Devil, with the Word of God, and so should you.

The Word of God has power, folks. Hello. Peter put it this way ...

> "Grace and peace be multiplied unto you through the knowledge of God, and of Jesus our Lord, According as his divine power hath given unto us all things that pertain unto life and godliness, through the knowledge of him that hath called us to glory and virtue: Whereby are given unto us exceeding great and precious promises: that by these ye might be partakers of the divine nature, having escaped the corruption that is in the world through lust."
>
> – 2 Pet. 1:2-4 (KJV)

The writer of Hebrews says the Word is sharper than a sword.

"For the word of God is quick, and

> powerful, and sharper than any twoedged sword, piercing even to the dividing asunder of soul and spirit, and of the joints and marrow, and is a discerner of the thoughts and intents of the heart."
>
> – Heb. 4:12 (KJV)

That's why Satan wants you to be an idiot swordsman – ignorant of the Word of God – because Christ's Word in your mouth mixed with a summit-or-plummet faith is a flippin' nightmare for the Nefarious One.

Look what the apostle Paul said about the Word of God coming out of your mouth ...

> "... The word is nigh thee, even in thy mouth, and in thy heart: that is, the word of faith, which we preach; That if thou shalt confess with thy mouth the Lord Jesus, and shalt believe in thine heart that God hath raised him from the dead, thou shalt be saved. For with the heart man believeth unto righteousness; and with the mouth confession is made unto salvation."
>
> – Rom. 10:8-10 (KJV)

Incredible. Believe and speak and boom ... God goes to work in your life. Not only in saving our sin-cursed souls but with regard to all things that pertain to life and godliness.

So, yeah ... our words matter.

While everyone else is yapping about fear, doubt, death, and disaster you should declare from God's Word fearlessness, faith, life, and his kingdom come. Can you dig it? I knew you could.

Speak God's Word over your current dilemma and watch him go to work kicking butt and taking names for his glory and on your behalf.

Agree with God's promises instead of the fear "The News" trades in.

Herewith are some glorious promises, in several categories, that you should start shouting from the rooftops, ASAP.

I've personalized these passages because oftentimes when we read 'em we don't get that even though they were about someone else many moons ago they're also given for *our* instruction and hope. Check it out ...

> For whatever was written in earlier times [in the Old Testament] was written for our instruction, so that through perseverance

and the encouragement of the Scriptures we might have hope.

– Rom. 15:4 (NASB)

The scriptures are given to encourage us, fill us with hope, and make us gritty with perseverance. Hello.

To feed and fuel the overcomer's spirit within you my brothers and sisters, I've divided up the diet herein to cover three spiritual food groups:

1. The Wealth

2. The Walk;

3. The Warfare of the Christian.

The Wealth proclamations are for the Christian to declare how spiritually rich they are in Christ.

The Walk proclamations are for the Christian to declare how they will biblically go against the grain of this corrupt culture.

The Warfare proclamations are for the Christian to declare their victory, in Christ, over all the works of the devil.

Keep this book handy, refer to it often, and buy five extra copies for your buddies who are going through a rough patch in life right now.

Our Wealth In Christ.

Proclamation #1. God Will Crush My Enemies.

> *"Satan's greatest weapon is man's ignorance of God's Word."*
>
> – A.W. Tozer

Is the enemy attacking you? In addition, are you getting sick of the onslaught of evil smacking our nation? If you answered "yes" to both of those inquiries then you should read this.

In 2 Chronicles 20:1-30, King Jehoshaphat and the people of God learned that three massive enemy tribes were looking to destroy the children of

Israel in the near future. As you can imagine, this info caused Jehoshaphat to freak out. Even though this 411 greatly disturbed the king, Jehoshaphat didn't allow his angst to make him morph into a hamster but rather he turned his attention to seek God. And God, as he is known to do, whipped Judah and Jerusalem's enemies in dramatic fashion while the people of God did nothing but sing and shout praises to God.

If you're worth your salt, you're going to get assaulted by the powers of darkness.

In addition, because of our nation's great Christian heritage, Satan isn't too chipper about those foundations standing, *ergo* ... he's going to try to lay waste to our land with his satanic devices.

So, what's the Christian to do? Cry? Complain? Eat a whole bottle of Tums? No, the believer should turn their attention to God and trust in him to eternally spank, in real-time, the evil forces leveled against us as individuals and our great land.

The following proclamation was cobbled together by me for you to pray with testicular fortitude against Satan and his ilk that seek to do you harm. Pray it with boldness. Pray it out loud.

I Talk Back to the Devil

Have your entire Bible study and/or church pray this in unison, with faith and attitude, and watch God begin his holy butt-kicking of devils attacking your life and those set against our nation.

Here's the proclamation. Remember, declare it out loud with attitude.

IN THE NAME OF JESUS, when the enemy comes against me, I will not give into dread and unbelief, but will instead turn my attention to seeking help from the Lord God Almighty who has sworn to uphold his people in dire straits.

And I am not praying to some pipsqueak little "g" god, but to the True God, the Ruler of the Kings of the Earth. Who rules kingdoms and nations and who has crushed Satan and his minions by Christ's death, burial, resurrection, and ascension. Who parted the Red Sea for Moses and raised Lazarus from the dead. I now ask you, Almighty God, to show your power as I am under attack by the enemy. I need your help now, hear my prayer and rescue me. Do not let the enemy take from me your blessings and our covenant birthrights. Crush every demon coming after me. I cannot defeat them on my own, but I am not on my own because you are forever with me, and you, O God, can and will turn them into snail slime.

In Jesus's name, I will not fear or worry about the attack that is now arrayed against me. This battle is not my battle, it is God's battle. I will stand and watch the Eternal God show up in my temporal mess and sort it out on my behalf for his glory. I totally trust that God is with me, therefore, I will praise him by singing with a loud voice and shouting your high praises.

I thank you, Lord, that this is not about my abilities but your divine power, and by your divine power, I will succeed when I trust in you and not in myself.

I declare in Jesus's name that when I trust in God and sing his high praises, God'll rout my enemies and put them into great confusion and then crush 'em like a worm. Not only will the enemy's attack fail but God'll richly bless me where the enemy intended to destroy me. In Jesus's name, amen!

I Talk Back to the Devil

Proclamation #2. God Will Bless Me with Holy Growth.

> *"When the devil sees a man or woman who really believes in prayer, who knows how to pray, and who really does pray, and, above all, when he sees a whole church on its face before God in prayer, he trembles as much as he ever did, for he knows that his day in that church or community is at an end."*
>
> – R.A. Torrey

"Blessed is the man that walketh not in the counsel of the ungodly, nor standeth in the way of sinners, nor sitteth in the seat of the scornful. But his delight is in the law of the Lord; and in his law doth he meditate day and night. And he shall be like a tree planted by the rivers of water, that bringeth forth his fruit in his season; his leaf also shall not wither; and whatsoever he doeth shall prosper.

The ungodly are not so: but are like the chaff which the wind driveth away. Therefore the ungodly shall not stand in the judgment, nor sinners in the congregation of the righteous. For the Lord knoweth the way of the righteous: but the way of the ungodly shall perish."

– Ps. 1:1-6 (KJV)

What a great passage of scripture. Now, let's make it our own prayer. Are you ready? Let's roll. Remember to declare it with faith, out loud, with maximum attitude.

FATHER, I DECLARE, in the mighty name of Jesus, that your favor will follow me when I don't listen to godless schemers, or bird-dog those who delight in filth, or take advice from clowns loaded down with bad ideas.

I Talk Back to the Devil

In Jesus's name, I proclaim that your Word is my delight and your Word is my focus from sun-up to sundown. Indeed, it is what I feast upon day and night.

By the power of the Holy Spirit, I will be a fruit-bearing tree for the kingdom of God and not some barren and vapid Christian tumbleweed. I will bear fruit that glorifies you. My leaves won't fade and whatever I do for your glory will prosper, in Jesus's name.

Through Christ's righteousness, his sacrifice for me, and my faith in him, I declare that I am not at all like the wicked who are dust in the wind, who are without defense at your judgment seat, and who are a bad influence upon your church.

In addition, Lord, I proclaim that you are my compass. You chart my course and you keep me off the wicked's highway to hell and for that, I give you praise, in Jesus's mighty name, amen!

Proclamation #3. When The Enemy Says, "You're Cursed" Shout This To Him.

> *"Each time, before you intercede, be quiet first, and worship God in His glory. Think of what He can do, and how He delights to hear the prayers of His redeemed people. Think of your place and privilege in Christ and expect great things!"*
>
> – Andrew Murray

"Today I am giving you the commands of the Lord your God. You must be careful to obey all of them completely. If you do that, he will make you greater than any other nation of people in the world.

Doug Giles

If you obey the Lord your God, he will bless you in very many ways.

God will bless you in your cities and in your fields.

God will bless your children and the crops that you grow. Your cows and your sheep will have many babies.

God will bless you with lots of grain to make bread.

God will bless you in your homes and when you go outside.

When your enemies attack you, the Lord will knock them down. They will come from one direction to attack you, but they will run away from you in seven different directions!

The Lord will bless you with lots of food to store. He will bless all the work that you do. He will bless you very much in the land that he is giving to you.

The Lord will continue to help you as his special people, as he has promised to do. But you must obey his commands. You must live in a way that pleases him. If you

I Talk Back to the Devil

do that, everyone in the world will see that you belong to the Lord. They will respect you with fear. The Lord will give you many children. Your animals will have many babies. Your fields will give you a lot of food. The Lord will do this in the land that he promised your ancestors he would give you.

The Lord will send rain from the clouds where he stores it. He will cause the rain to fall at the time when the land needs it. He will bless all the work that you do. You will lend money to the people of many nations. But you will not need anyone to lend money to you. The Lord will make you the leaders of other people. You will not have to follow at the back. You will become more powerful, not weaker. But you must obey the commands of the Lord your God. I am telling you today, you must be very careful to do that. You must continue to obey all the commands that I am giving you today. Do not turn away from them to do anything else. Do not try to worship other gods."

– Deuteronomy 28:1-14 (EASY)

Shout the following out loud!

HEAVENLY FATHER, I thank you that in Christ Jesus, through the blood of the new covenant, I am blessed with every spiritual blessing. Holy Spirit, incline my ear to listen closely to the Word of God and to cherish your commandments.

Lift me high above all the garbage that tries to drag me back into sin and unbelief.

I declare that instead of a crummy walk with God filled with compromise and defeat, your blessings will chase me down as I follow you wholeheartedly.

Everywhere I go, your favor will follow me.

In addition, you will bless my kids and you will bless all my righteous enterprises.

You will grace my coming and going.

When my enemies attack me they'll have to contend with you and you're no one to be messed with. You will hammer my enemies so hard they'll splinter off in seven different directions.

I am so grateful and thankful for your divine favor over me and that I belong to you in a special way that I do not deserve, but you chose to love me anyway.

Thank you, Lord, for giving more than enough in this life. Guide me, Oh God, to use these resources to establish Your kingdom.

Thank you, Lord, that your blessings upon me will be so abundant that I won't have to beg, borrow or steal.

I declare in the name of Jesus, by the Holy Spirit, that I will triumph over my flesh and every demon power that is set against me.

Lord God, keep my heart running towards your commandments and not deviating to the right or the left, and make me despise all forms of idolatry in Jesus's name, amen!

Proclamation #4. This Proclamation Will Light Wet Wood.

> *"You can do more than pray after you have prayed, but you cannot do more than pray until you have prayed. Pray often, for prayer is a shield to the soul, a sacrifice to God, and a scourge to Satan."*
>
> – John Bunyan

I've personalized this proclamation for the believer from Paul's first chapter of his letter to the Ephesians (Eph 1:1-23) using The Message Translation.

Doug Giles

This is to be read out loud, with testicular fortitude, especially if you're feeling a wee bit crappy today. Enjoy and let 'er rip. You're welcome.

I, _____ (add your name), am under God's plan as a _____ (add your calling), I'm a special agent of Christ Jesus.

Grace and peace have been poured into my life by God our Father and our Master, Jesus Christ.

How blessed is God! And what a blessing you are, Lord!

You are the Father of our Master, Jesus Christ, and you take me to the high places of blessing in him.

Long before he laid down Earth's foundations, he had me in mind, had settled on me as the focus of his love, to be made whole and holy by his love.

Long, long ago, he decided to adopt me into his family through Jesus Christ. (What pleasure he took in planning this!) He wanted me to enter into the celebration of his lavish gift-giving by the hand of his beloved Son.

Because of the sacrifice of the Messiah, his

blood poured out on the altar of the Cross, I'm a free person, free of penalties and punishments chalked up by all my misdeeds. And not just barely free, either. *Abundantly* free!

He thought of everything, provided for everything I could possibly need, letting me in on the plans he took such delight in making.

He set it all out before us in Christ, a long-range plan in which everything would be brought together and summed up in him, everything in deepest Heaven, everything on planet Earth. It's in Christ that I find out who I am and what I am living for.

Long before I first heard of Christ and got my hopes up, he had his eye on me, had designs on me for glorious living, part of the overall purpose he is working out in everything and everyone.

It's in Christ that once I heard the truth and believed it (this Message of my salvation), found myself home free – signed, sealed, and delivered by the Holy Spirit.

This down payment from God is the first installment on what's coming, a reminder that I'll get everything God has planned for me, a praising and glorious life.

I ask – ask the God of our Master, Jesus Christ, the God of glory – to make me intelligent and discerning in knowing him personally, my eyes focused and clear, so that I can see exactly what it is he is calling me to do, grasp the immensity of this glorious way of life he has for "his" me, oh, the utter extravagance of his work for those who trust him – endless energy, boundless strength!

All this energy issues from Christ: God raised him from death and set him on a throne in deep Heaven, in charge of running the universe, everything from galaxies to governments; no name and no power exempt from his rule.

And not just for the time being, but *forever*. He is in charge of it all, has the final word on everything. At the center of all this, Christ rules the church. The church, you see, is not peripheral to the world; the world is peripheral to the church. The church is Christ's body, in which he speaks and acts, by which he fills everything with his presence.

I Talk Back to the Devil

Proclamation #5. When Buried Under A Mountain of Sin, God'll Show Me Grace.

> *"My main ambition in life is to be on the devil's most wanted list."*
>
> – Leonard Ravenhill

This is a glorious chunk of scripture. Every time the powers of darkness tell you you're "unworthy" tell them thanks for the reminder because Jesus died for the unworthy and then shout this proclamation at them.

Doug Giles

"And you were dead in your trespasses and sins, in which you formerly walked according to the course of this world, according to the prince of the power of the air, of the spirit that is now working in the sons of disobedience. Among them we too all formerly lived in the lusts of our flesh, indulging the desires of the flesh and of the mind, and were by nature children of wrath, even as the rest. But God, being rich in mercy, because of His great love with which He loved us, even when we were dead in our transgressions, made us alive together with Christ (by grace you have been saved), and raised us up with him, and seated us with him in the heavenly places in Christ Jesus, so that in the ages to come He might show the surpassing riches of His grace in kindness toward us in Christ Jesus. For by grace you have been saved through faith; and that not of yourselves, it is the gift of God; not as a result of works, so that no one may boast. For we are His workmanship, created in Christ Jesus for good works, which God prepared beforehand so that we would walk in them."

– Ephesians 2:1-10 (NASB)

I Talk Back to the Devil

HEAVENLY FATHER, I thank you and give you praise that when I was dead in my sins and enslaved to this perverted world, joyfully following demonic spirits, being utterly disobedient to you, indulging deeply in the desires of the flesh and the mind, and was, by my very nature a child of wrath, that you showed me mercy instead of judgment.

Indeed, Lord, you showed me your unfathomable richness of your love and mercy and you united me with your Holy Son and gave my broken soul his holy life. Yes, when I was buried under a mountain of sin you showed me grace and I am forever grateful to you!

Not only did you salvage my soul but you also raised me with Jesus and have seated me in heavenly places with him right now.

My prayer, O God, is that my life will be a living testimony of the surpassing richness of your amazing grace and incredible kindness that you freely gave to me in Christ Jesus.

I will always declare that it was by your grace that I was saved.

I received that gift by faith and not works!

My salvation had nothing to do with me. It was not my plan and it didn't come about by my efforts. I did not earn it. It was the gift of God, pure and simple. Now I am your workmanship created in Christ Jesus to accomplish good works which you Lord arranged to occur a long, long time ago.

I thank you, Father, for your amazing love in Jesus's name, amen!

I Talk Back to the Devil

Proclamation #6. God Will Float My Financial Boat.

> *"We are evidently no friends of Satan. Like the kings of this world, he wars not against his own subjects. The very fact that he assaults us should fill our minds with hope."*
>
> – J. C. Ryle

For those folks freaking out over finances, digest these scriptures and then belt out this proclamation of God's great faithfulness to provide for his people.

"Therefore take no thought, saying, What shall we eat? or, What shall we drink? or, Wherewithal shall we be clothed? (For after all these things do the Gentiles seek:) for your heavenly Father knoweth that ye have need of all these things. But seek ye first the kingdom of God, and his righteousness; and all these things shall be added unto you. Take therefore no thought for the morrow: for the morrow shall take thought for the things of itself. Sufficient unto the day is the evil thereof."

– Matthew. 6:31-34 (KJV)

"And God is able to make all grace abound toward you; that ye, always having all sufficiency in all things, may abound to every good work: (As it is written, He hath dispersed abroad; he hath given to the poor: his righteousness remaineth forever. Now he that ministereth seed to the sower both minister bread for your food, and multiply your seed sown, and increase the fruits of your righteousness;) Being enriched in every thing to all bountifulness, which causeth through us thanksgiving to God."

– 2Cor. 9: 8-11 (KJV)

I Talk Back to the Devil

"Trust in the Lord with all your heart And do not lean on your own understanding. In all your ways acknowledge Him, and He will make your paths straight. Do not be wise in your own eyes; Fear the Lord and turn away from evil. It will be healing to your body and refreshment to your bones. Honor the Lord from your wealth And from the first of all your produce; So your barns will be filled with plenty And your vats will overflow with new wine."

– Proverbs 3:5-10 (NASB)

Alright, here we go. Are you ready? Remember to proclaim these with gusto. Let's roll.

IN THE MIGHTY NAME OF JESUS, I will not cave into fear regarding finances. If God takes care of birds and flowers he'll definitely take care of my financial well-being. God will attend to me, do his best for me and uphold me financially. I will not be like a pagan who does not know God and is preoccupied with getting cash instead of pursuing the Lord. My focus is on God's kingdom business. I know how he works. I seek his will, I build his kingdom, I long for his righteousness and he will supply all of my earthly needs.

Not only will the Lord meet my basic needs but he will pour out his blessings upon me in astonishing ways so that I'll be ready for anything that comes my way. God will bless me financially so that I can sow that money into the kingdom of God and wreck hell's habitations. The money that God has richly blessed me with will go towards establishing his covenant in the earth and not to silly garbage.

So when it comes to money, I proclaim I will trust God with all my heart and not try to figure everything out. I will follow his lead and not this world's mindset. I declare that I will honor God with everything I have and give him the best of the best and not scraps and that in turn he will burst my barns and flood my wine vats, in Jesus's mighty name, amen!

I Talk Back to the Devil

Proclamation #7. The Name of The Lord Is A Strong Tower - Declare It!

> *"Satan so hates the genuine praise of Christ that his fiery darts of discouragement are not effective against us when we respond in praise."*
>
> – William Thrasher

Pastors nowadays refer to Jesus as one's "personal Savior".

How quaint, eh?

In Psalm 59, David, being the constantly in

trouble child of God that he was, saw God not just as some amorphous "personal Savior" but referred to God as ...

1. Lord God of Hosts – "Hosts" means "angelic armies." – v. 5

2. The God of my mercy. – v. 10

3. O Lord our Shield. – v. 11

4. The God who rules to the ends of the earth. – v. 15

5. God of my defense. – v. 17

Matter of fact, David had a litany of names and descriptions for the Shepherd of his soul throughout the Psalms. Shout these out to God at the top of your lungs when the enemy is attacking you, the Church, our families, and our great nation. God's a holy butt-kicker against all that is evil and the clowns who're attached to Satan's devices.

Proclaim his various names out loud with some gusto!

- Names of God in the book of Psalms
- The Lord – 1:2

I Talk Back to the Devil

- The God of my righteousness – 4:1
- My King – 5:2
- Lord my God – 7:1
- The God of my salvation – 18:46
- The God of Jacob – 20:1
- My Strength – 22:19
- The King of glory – 29:3
- Lord God of Truth – 31:5
- The Lord God of Israel – 41:13
- Mighty One – 45:3
- The King of all the earth – 47:7
- The God of Abraham – 47:9
- God Most High – 57:2
- YAHWEH – 68:4
- The Almighty – 68:14
- God the Lord – 68:20
- Holy One of Israel – 71:22
- Shepherd of Israel – 80:1
- The Lord our Maker – 95:6

- God their Savior – 106:21
- The Mighty One of Jacob – 132:2
- The God of gods – 136:2
- The God of heaven – 136:26

Descriptions of God in the book of Psalms

- A shield for me – 3:3
- My glory – 3:3
- The one who lifts up my head – 3:3
- The righteous God – 7:9
- A just judge – 7:11
- A refuge – 9:9
- The portion of my inheritance and my cup – 16:5
- My strength – 18:1
- My rock and my fortress and my deliverer – 18:2
- The horn of my salvation, stronghold – 18:2
- My support – 18:18
- My shepherd – 23:1
- My light and my salvation – 27:1

I Talk Back to the Devil

- The strength of my life – 27:1
- The saving refuge of his anointed – 28:8
- My helper – 30:10
- The rock of refuge – 31:2
- My hiding place – 32:7
- My help and my deliverer – 41:17
- The God of my life – 42:8
- My exceeding joy – 43:4
- A very present help in trouble – 46:1
- Our guide even to death – 48:14
- My defense – 59:9
- My God of mercy – 59:10
- A shelter for me, a strong tower from the enemy – 61:3
- A father of the fatherless, a defender of widows – 68:5
- The strength of my heart and my portion forever – 73:26
- The great God and the great King above all gods – 95:3
- He who keeps Israel – 121:4

- My shade at my right hand – 121:5
- My portion in the land of the living – 142:5
- My high tower – 144:2

Work those titles and descriptions of God into your fervent prayers and into your worship and watch what God does to the powers of darkness when they try to assail you.

I Talk Back to the Devil

Proclamation #8. I Am A Friend of God.

> *"When a Christian shuns fellowship with other Christians, the devil smiles. When he stops studying the Bible, the devil laughs. When he stops praying, the devil shouts for joy."*
>
> – Corrie Ten Boom

Before any person becomes a Christian they are an enemy of God. Yep, before the regeneration of the person, by the Holy Spirit, they are openly hostile to the Holy One.

Awww … what's the matter?

Did mommy not tell you that growing up? Did mommy tell you that you were a sweet little angel? If yes, mommy was wrong. Every person, outside of Christ, is an enemy of God and God's their worst nightmare.

Paul put it this way …

> "And you were dead in your trespasses and sins, in which you formerly walked according to the course of this world, according to the prince of the power of the air, of the spirit that is now working in the sons of disobedience. Among them we too all formerly lived in the lusts of our flesh, indulging the desires of the flesh and of the mind, and were by nature children of wrath, even as the rest."
>
> – Ephesians 2:1-3 (NASB)

And he put our inglorious state this way here in Romans Three …

> "… both Jews and Greeks are all under sin; as it is written, "There is none righteous, not even one; There is none who understands, There is none who seeks for God; All have turned aside, together they have become

useless; There is none who does good, There is not even one.""Their throat is an open grave, With their tongues they keep deceiving," "The poison of asps is under their lips"; "Whose mouth is full of cursing and bitterness"; "Their feet are swift to shed blood, Destruction and misery are in their paths, And the path of peace they have not known." "There is no fear of God before their eyes."

– Romans 3: 9-18 (NASB).

Brutal, eh? You won't hear those two sets of scripture quoted at Joel Osteen's church, but there they sit … bigger than Dallas … and dire in their denunciations of the dude or dudette in a pre-salvific state.

Some people would deem those texts as "rude" or "negative". I deem them as a "refreshing and necessary" acid bath of truth needed to wake the sinner up to their impending doom outside of Christ. The revelation of our damnable condition makes God's grace amazing and his mercy magnificent when it's applied to the sinners account via Jesus's sacrificial death for his elect. To the believer, by Christ's finished work on the cross, our sin debt is settled and the war between us and God is over.

Or as Paul put it …

> "But now in Christ Jesus you who formerly were far off have been brought near by the blood of Christ. For He Himself is our peace, who made both groups into one and broke down the barrier of the dividing wall, by abolishing in His flesh the enmity, which is the Law of commandments contained in ordinances, so that in Himself He might make the two into one new man, thus establishing peace, and might reconcile them both in one body to God through the cross, by it having put to death the enmity."
>
> – Ephesians 2:13-16 (NASB)

"For while we were still helpless, at the right time Christ died for the ungodly. For one will hardly die for a righteous man; though perhaps for the good man someone would dare even to die. But God demonstrates His own love toward us, in that while we were yet sinners, Christ died for us. Much more then, having now been justified by His blood, we shall be saved from the wrath of God through Him. For if while we were enemies we were reconciled to God through the death of His Son, much

> more, having been reconciled, we shall be saved by His life. And not only this, but we also exult in God through our Lord Jesus Christ, through whom we have now received the reconciliation."
>
> – Romans 5:6-11 (NASB)

After Jesus brings us into his fold by his sacrifice and his doing we are no longer estranged enemies of God under his wrath but now the Christian is a child of God and a friend of God. Holy cow. We were once sworn enemies and now God calls us friends! That's beautiful, man and no matter how we feel, we need to declare that he calls us his friend now.

Check it out ...

> "Greater love has no one than this, that one lay down his life for his friends. You are My friends if you do what I command you. No longer do I call you slaves, for the slave does not know what his master is doing; but I have called you friends, for all things that I have heard from My Father I have made known to you."
>
> – John 15:13-15 (NASB)

Let's proclaim the fact that we are friends with God and it isn't based upon our performance but on Jesus's sacrifice on our behalf.

Here we go … shout the following out at the top of your lungs.

LORD, I PROCLAIM, in your Son's mighty name, that I am your friend and not your enemy.

The war between us is over.

The enmity between us is over.

I am not a child of this world, controlled by evil spirits, totally disobedient, living for lusts, a veritable child of wrath.

That old me is dead in Christ.

The new me lives for your will, I'm controlled by the Holy Spirit, you've given me an obedient heart and I'm now a product of your amazing grace.

By the blood of Jesus, even though I was far away from God, Jesus has now brought me near to him.

Now he is my peace. Through him I am reconciled. And by him our feud is over.

I Talk Back to the Devil

I am saved from the wrath of God.

I am reconciled to the Lord and now, by Christ's doing, he calls me his friend!

I. Am. A. Friend. Of. God.

* Let that sink in. Ain't it glorious? Give him a shout of praise and thanksgiving ...

Proclamation #9. Your Identity in Christ.

> *"Do not be despondent when fighting against the incorporeal enemy, but even in the midst of your afflictions and oppression praise the Lord, Who has found you worthy to suffer for Him, by struggling against the subtlety of the serpent, and to be wounded for Him at every hour; for had you not lived piously, and endeavored to become united to God, the enemy would not have attacked and tormented you."*
>
> – John of Kronstadt

You're about to have your mind blown. What the scripture states about the born again believer is incredible. You might not "feel" the following but the scripture declares it is real for the true Christian. So, instead of declaring what yo' mamma says about you or what Instagram says about you or what judgy religious people say about you, why not, from here on out, declare what God says about you in Christ Jesus.

I personalized the following so that the reader will understand God means you. These truths are for you. Remember to declare these proclamations out loud with attitude.

IN CHRIST, I am loved, chosen, forgiven, redeemed, and adopted by God Almighty through the sacrifice of his beloved Son and I'm not a barely saved and lonely weirdo but a living, breathing, demon-crushing, on-fire born of God's Spirit summit-or-plummet Christian wrecking-crane to Satan's devices. .

GOD made his Son who had no sin to be sin for me, so that in him I might become the righteousness of God. –2 Cor. 5:21 (NIV)

I Talk Back to the Devil

IN CHRIST, I am God's handiwork, born again to do good works, which God prepared in advance for me to do. These preordained good works will destroy the forces of darkness and salvage broken people and glorify my Father in Heaven – Eph. 2:10 (NIV)

IN CHRIST, I am a new creation. The old me is gone, it's toast, it's been murdered and buried and the new me is here ready to glorify God!" – 2 Cor. 5:17 (NIV)

IN CHRIST, I am no longer a foreigner and stranger, but I am a fellow citizen with God's people and also a member of his household. – Eph. 2:19 (NIV)

IN CHRIST, God is able to bless me abundantly, so that in all things at all times, having all that I need, I will abound in every good work. – 2 Cor. 9:8 (NIV)

IN CHRIST, great love from the Father has been lavished on me, that I should be called a child of God! And that is what I am! – 1 John 3:1 (NIV)

IN CHRIST, the LORD my God is with me, the Mighty Warrior who saves. He will take great delight in me; in his love he will no longer rebuke me, but will rejoice over me with singing. – Zeph 3:17 (NIV)

That was pretty awesome, eh? But wait! There's more!

Look what the blood of Jesus has afforded the believer. (The following is paraphrased from a Rick Godwin sermon).

Say with me ...

LORD JESUS, I make this proclamation in faith believing that I have overcome Satan when I testify personally to what the Word of God says that the blood of Jesus does for me.

Through the blood of Jesus, I am redeemed out of the hand of the devil. – Rev.12:11

Through the blood of Jesus, all my sins are forgiven. – Eph.1:7

Through the blood of Jesus, I am continually being cleansed from all sin. – 1Jn.1:9

Through the blood of Jesus, I am justified. I am made righteous ... just as if I'd never sinned. – 1Jn.1:7

I Talk Back to the Devil

Through the blood of Jesus, I am made holy and set apart to God – Heb.13:12

Through the blood of Jesus, there is no condemnation to those who are in Christ Jesus. – Rom.8:1

Through the blood of Jesus, I have boldness to enter into the presence of God. – Heb.10:19.

Through the blood of Jesus, Christ himself is in heaven interceding on my behalf. – Heb.7:15.

Through the blood of Jesus, he not only forgives my sins but heals my diseases. – 1Pet.2:24.

Through the blood of Jesus, Satan has no place in me, no power over me, and no claims against me. It's all been settled at the cross. – Rev.12:11.

Through the blood of Jesus, I am free. – Jn.8:36

Thank you, Lord God! Thank you, Lord God, for such a great salvation!

» *Dog-ear this chapter and refer back to it quite often and shout out who God declares you to be when the devil, culture, and legalistic religious dorks try to saddle you with shame and condemnation.*

Proclamation #10. Psalm 112 - God's Blessings Upon Your Kids

> *"Prayer is repeating the victor's name (Jesus) into the ears of Satan and insisting on his retreat."*
>
> – S.D. Gordon

Dear Christian: If you have kids you need to cling to this promise from God like stink clings to a monkey. Check out King Jimmy's Version of Psalm 112 …

Doug Giles

Praise ye the Lord. Blessed is the man that feareth the Lord, that delighteth greatly in his commandments.

His seed shall be mighty upon earth: the generation of the upright shall be blessed.

Wealth and riches shall be in his house: and his righteousness endureth for ever.

Unto the upright there ariseth light in the darkness: he is gracious, and full of compassion, and righteous.

A good man sheweth favour, and lendeth: he will guide his affairs with discretion.

Surely he shall not be moved for ever: the righteous shall be in everlasting remembrance.

He shall not be afraid of evil tidings: his heart is fixed, trusting in the Lord.

His heart is established, he shall not be afraid, until he see his desire upon his enemies.

He hath dispersed, he hath given to the poor; his righteousness endureth for ever; his horn shall be exalted with honour.

I Talk Back to the Devil

> The wicked shall see it, and be grieved; he shall gnash with his teeth, and melt away: the desire of the wicked shall perish.

Alright. Let's proclaim this with gusto.

HEAVENLY FATHER, your Word declares that the man or woman who fears you is blessed. So I am asking, O Lord, to give me that heart that fears you and not men, devils, or culture. Indeed, give me a heart that desires your way and your commandments.

Father, I declare, according to your Word, your covenant promises, that my kids will be holy, robust believers on the earth and that my house will be blessed and their houses will be filled with true riches.

Lord, I proclaim that my kids will grow up to be generous givers and not self-obsessed me-monkeys.

Let your light always shine upon my kids as they walk in your grace, mercy, and justice. Establish them with a solid, God-glorifying reputations where they are undaunted by gossip and smack-talking enemies.

Establish my children, Lord, as solid rocks in your kingdom, fully devoted to you, ever blessed by you, and unfazed at whatever hell throws at them. Grant them a life of blessing and honor that drives the powers of darkness nuts. In Jesus's name, amen!

I Talk Back to the Devil

Our Walk in Christ.

Proclamation #11. I'm Dead to My Flesh and Alive to God.

> *"All the cunning of the devil is exercised in trying to tear us away from the word."*
>
> – Martin Luther

"But I say, walk by the Spirit, and you will not carry out the desire of the flesh. For the flesh sets its desire against the Spirit, and the Spirit against the flesh; for these are in opposition to one another, so that you may not do the things that you please. But if you are led by the Spirit, you are not under the

Law. Now the deeds of the flesh are evident, which are: immorality, impurity, sensuality, idolatry, sorcery, enmities, strife, jealousy, outbursts of anger, disputes, dissensions, factions, envying, drunkenness, carousing, and things like these, of which I forewarn you, just as I have forewarned you, that those who practice such things will not inherit the kingdom of God. But the fruit of the Spirit is love, joy, peace, patience, kindness, goodness, faithfulness, gentleness, self-control; against such things there is no law. Now those who belong to Christ Jesus have crucified the flesh with its passions and desires."

– Galatians 5:16-24 (NASB)

Dear Christian: Before any demons kick you in the teeth this morning declare this prayer. Yep, tell your flesh to go pound sand and proclaim you're going to walk in the Spirit this day and everyday forward, by God's grace, for his glory, in Jesus's name.

Remember, shout this proclamation out loud and do it so loud that it scares yo' mamma. Enjoy and share.

I Talk Back to the Devil

IN THE NAME OF JESUS, I will walk in the Spirit and I'll let the Spirit of the living God order my life.

In the name of Jesus, I'm not going to give in to my selfish and sinful desires.

In the name of Jesus, I am not subject to the flesh, or the law and the death that they bring, but instead I am Spirit-led.

In the name of Jesus, I put to death corrupt sexual relationships, porn, impurity, and lust.

In the name of Jesus, I put to death idolatry, witchcraft, hatred, arguing, jealousy, anger, selfishness, contentiousness, and division.

In the name of Jesus, I put to death envy of others' well-being, drunkenness, and all shameful behavior that plagues humanity.

In the name of Jesus, I will not give way to these soul-damning deeds.

In the name of Jesus, I will walk in the Spirit and produce the following fruits thirty, sixty, and one hundred fold for his glory.

In the name of Jesus, I will exhibit unconditional love, joy, peace, patience, kindness, goodness, and faithfulness, gentleness and self control.

In the name of Jesus, I belong to Christ and my flesh is a dead man. My lusts and wicked desires will no longer plague me.

In the name of Jesus, I choose to walk in the Spirit, and by his power, I will keep in sync with the Spirit of the Living God.

In the name of Jesus, I am bold, wild, and free to follow him and not my filthy flesh, in Jesus's name, amen.

I Talk Back to the Devil

Proclamation #12. Blessed Are You When People Insult You.

> *"Christians are to pray for the manifestation of the reign of Christ and the emergence of His kingdom."*
>
> – R.C. Sproul

> "Blessed are you when people insult you, persecute you and falsely say all kinds of evil against you because of me. Rejoice and be glad, because great is your reward in heaven, for in the same way they persecuted the prophets who were before you.
>
> – Matthew 5:11-12 (NIV)

Here's a blessing a lot of Christians don't pray for namely, the "blessing" of people talking mad smack about them and their commitment to Christ. It doesn't feel like a blessing when you're getting jet-blasted by folks behind your back, or to your face, or online by the anonymous cowards that proliferate social media, but Jesus declared, contrary to what it feels like, that the one under attack for following him is a very blessed *amigo*.

By the way, most of Jesus's grief, David's pain and Paul's persecution came through the pieholes of religious people. Yep, the sanctimonious hoity-toity were the vessels of vomit that attacked the Son of God, the prophets, and the apostles ninety-plus percent of the time. So, don't think it's weird when the religious rage against you. They're children of the Devil, the father of lies, the source of slander, libel, accusation, and condemnation and that's all they have to do is to gossip and malign Christians who're following the Rebel from Galilee.

If people are talking twaddle about your biblical stance then please, declare this with me now …

I Talk Back to the Devil

IN JESUS'S MIGHTY NAME, the persecution that I'm currently undergoing for Christ's sake is a big ... big ... big-time blessing.

Thank you, Lord, that I get to suffer your name's sake.

I proclaim that I am blessed and not cursed every time people put me down, or exclude me, or speak lies about me, and seek to discredit me.

Just because they're uncomfortable with the truth and it's hitting them too close to home that doesn't make me the bad guy.

I will not mourn when this occurs to me but I will be glad when they set their mouths against me.

Indeed, I will shout for joy because even though they don't like my stance on biblical truth, you do, Lord God, and that's all that matters.

According to the Word of God, heaven applauds my fidelity to the Scripture when it isn't easy.

I declare what Jesus said that when I am under the gun for gospel reasons that I am in good company with the ancient prophets who were always getting into this type of trouble.

Thank you for this blessing, Father, in Jesus's name, amen!

I Talk Back to the Devil

Proclamation #13. God Hates This Type of Person - Don't Be Like Them.

> *"To pray is to enter the treasure-house of God and to gather riches out of an inexhaustible storehouse."*
>
> – Charles Spurgeon

I wish I had a dollar for every time I've heard altruistic people say that "God loves everyone ... we're all God's children." Uh ... no we're not. If you need a little proof then check out this passage.

Doug Giles

"A worthless person, a wicked man,
Is the one who walks with a perverse mouth,
Who winks with his eyes, who signals with his feet,
Who points with his fingers;
Who with perversity in his heart continually devises evil,
Who spreads strife.
Therefore his calamity will come suddenly;
Instantly he will be broken and there will be no healing.
There are six things which the Lord hates,
Yes, seven which are an abomination to Him:
Haughty eyes, a lying tongue,
And hands that shed innocent blood,
A heart that devises wicked plans,
Feet that run rapidly to evil, A false witness who utters lies,
And one who spreads strife among brothers"

— Proverbs 6:12-19 (NASB)

Check it out …

I Talk Back to the Devil

If you're a constant liar. If you're a swindler and a grifter. If you're always thinking up fresh ways to con people and you spread strife and talk garbage about others everywhere you go, you're in big trouble with God. Verse fifteen of Proverbs six says that type of dude or dudette will be destroyed suddenly and broken beyond any hope of healing. Twice in eight verses here in Proverbs six, Solomon says a major trait that Jehovah hates is a person "who spreads strife among brothers. (Prov.6:14,19)

To circumvent becoming that which the Lord abhors, declare the following proclamations so that you will not loan your tongue to the Devil to be used for his demonic destruction amongst brothers and sisters.

Pray this with boldness out loud!

IN JESUS'S NAME, keep me, O Lord, from being dishonest, spreading strife, and separating close friends.

In Jesus's name, keep me, O Lord, from all corrupt talk.

In Jesus's name, keep me, O Lord, from disseminating or listening to gossip and slander.

In Jesus's name, keep me, O Lord, from speaking evil and deceit.

In Jesus's name, keep me, O Lord, from lying lips.

In Jesus's name, keep me, O Lord, from being an idle fool, a homewrecker, and a pathetic busybody.

In Jesus's name, keep me, O Lord, from quarreling, envy, anger, hostility, libel, gossip, conceit, and disorder.

In Jesus's name, keep me, O Lord, from an unbridled tongue.

In Jesus's name, keep me, O Lord, from broadcasting a false report and joining hands with a wicked man to be a malicious witness.

In Jesus's name, keep me, O Lord, from speaking evil of a brother.

In Jesus's name, keep me, O Lord, from secretly defaming people.

In Jesus's name, keep me, O Lord, from forgetting that Romans 1:29-32 states that gossipers have been given over to a depraved mind and deserve the death penalty.

I Talk Back to the Devil

In Jesus's name, keep me, O Lord, from letting the powers of darkness use my tongue, turning it into a fire of unrighteousness that sets my life aflame with the very fires of hell.

In Jesus's name, keep me, O Lord, from having a fool's mouth that ruins my life and snares my soul.

In Jesus's name, keep me, O Lord, from living an undignified life of backbiting people. Instead, make me sober-minded and faithful in all things.

In Jesus's name, keep me, O Lord, from finding gossip remotely appealing. Indeed, make me hate that garbage like you do. In Jesus's name, amen!

Proclamation #14. Speak The Word of God with Boldness.

> *"God answers prayer for the same reason He saves people, goodness shown in grace.*
>
> *— A.W. Tozer*

> *"And now, Lord, take note of their threats, and grant that Your bond-servants may speak Your word with all confidence, while You extend Your hand to heal, and signs and wonders take place through the name*

of Your holy servant Jesus." And when they had prayed, the place where they had gathered together was shaken, and they were all filled with the Holy Spirit and began to speak the word of God with boldness.

– Acts 4:29-31 (NASB)

In Acts chapter four, Peter and John got thrown in jail for preaching Jesus and the resurrection of the dead. The smarmy religious dweebs didn't like the fact that the Jesus they had just crucified rose from the dead and Peter and John weren't going to let them forget about it. The people, however, loved the message, the opportunity to repent, and the fact that God had shown them grace to believe. On that day alone, five thousand folks got saved. Can you say … #boom?!?

The point of this chapter/proclamation is Peter and John wouldn't back down from preaching the gospel when tossed in jail and commanded not to preach anymore. They couldn't care less if Zuckerberg banned them from Facebook. They wore the enemy's rage as a badge of honor. Today, more than ever, we need bold witnesses for Jesus and his Word in this adulterous and perverted generation. Yep, we need Christians with

I Talk Back to the Devil

cojones who will not fold like a cheap suit when pressured to shut up on the God talk.

If you need a good mega-dose of Holy Ghost boldness to speak biblical truth in godless environments, pray the following out loud and believe God to give you an epic dollop of what Peter and John enjoyed in Acts chapter four. Here we go ...

HEAVENLY FATHER, in the mighty name of Jesus, fill me with the Holy Spirit. The spirit of lion-like boldness ... to speak your Word ... unafraid ... with biblical clarity, authority, and with great conviction.

Lord God, make me unafraid to declare your truth, when called upon, no matter who likes it or not.

Take from my heart any fear of man. Help me, Oh Lord, to only fear you and you alone.

Let all threats of punishment, hatred, and intimidation from this culture roll off me like water off a duck's back.

Help me, Holy Spirit, not to be ashamed of you and your Word when I'm around whomever. Whether they are acquaintances ... or uppity religious dorks ... or an anti-Christian boss ... or nosy neighbors ... or evil gym rats ... or any and all naysayers and lie-peddlers.

Grant me, Lord, to never stop speaking about what I've seen and heard from you.

When I get persecuted for declaring your truth in a hostile environment, take note of their threats and grant me the power to speak your Word with all confidence.

In addition, Lord, do mighty miracles in the hearts and lives of those who're open to the gospel so that your Son is glorified and the enemies of the gospel are stupefied.

Anoint me, Lord, to be an effective witness everywhere I go.

Fill me with your Spirit and let me speak the Word of God with all boldness, in Jesus's name, amen!

I Talk Back to the Devil

Proclamation #15. Create In Me A Clean Heart.

> *"Prayer imparts the power to walk and not faint."*
>
> – Oswald Chambers

Have you ever blown it really badly and sinned against the Lord? No? Well la-di-da. Look at you … you're such an angel. Me, on the other hand … well … my halo has fallen off, unfortunately, many times. The truth is we all sin in many ways and if you don't think you do then you have two problems. Number One: You have a low view of God and Number Two: You have a high view of yourself.

King David blew it badly when he had an affair with Bathsheba and then had her husband Uriah murdered to cover his backside. This shattered David because he had drifted so far away from being the young, grateful, worshiping shepherd kid who loved God with all of his heart to become an adulterer and murderer. Whether or not you have committed the sins which David committed we all have experienced the painful consequences of following our flesh and listening to devils instead of the Holy Spirit.

That's where Psalm fifty-one comes into play. There's no telling how many millions of times this psalm has been turned to and prayed after God's chosen ones have messed up royally and were heartsick about it. I know I prayed this psalm many, many times. If you have screwed up, don't despair … just pray this prayer.

HEAVENLY FATHER, you are my Rock and my Fortress, please look on me with a heart of mercy, generous love, and your great compassion, and erase every repercussion of my shameful sins.

I Talk Back to the Devil

Lord God, I am asking you to thoroughly cleanse me from inside and out from all my wicked deeds and purge me of my sins.

Father, I am completely aware of how badly I've blown it. I make no excuses. I take full responsibility. My guilt stares me in the face.

It has been against you and only you that I have sinned and I have committed the very acts which your Word condemns.

Scrub the filth from my heart, Oh Lord. Wash me and make me white as snow. I want to once again know joy and happiness and dance in delight. But now … it feels like I've been run over by a train. Help me, God.

Erase my guilt from the record.

Create in me a clean heart. A heart that runs to you instead of sinful filth. Restore my first love for you. Make my heart once again headstrong for your ways. Buoy up my spirit, Lord.

Father, I'm asking you not to toss me away from your presence and not to remove the Holy Spirit from me like you did with King Saul.

If you do, I will spend my energy teaching sinners about you and leading them to Christ.

Free me from the stain of my sin, my Savior and my Redeemer.

Lord God, my tongue that was used for destruction I will turn and use it to sing your praises regarding your righteousness and justice.

Father, I would give up all my prized possessions to prove how sick I am for what I have done but you do not care about that stuff.

The only thing you're looking for is true brokenness: a smashed spirit and a heart that truly regrets past sins is the only thing you won't detest. That's what I give to you, O God, a broken spirit. Forgive and renew me, my Lord.

Thank you that there is no condemnation in Christ Jesus.

Thank you that when I fully own up to the evil I've done you are faithful to forgive me and purge me from the stain of all the bad things I have wrought. In Jesus's name, amen.

Here's the full Psalm 51 in the King James Version.

> Have mercy upon me, O God, according to thy lovingkindness: according unto the multitude of thy tender mercies blot out my transgressions. Wash me thoroughly from

I Talk Back to the Devil

mine iniquity, and cleanse me from my sin.

For I acknowledge my transgressions: and my sin is ever before me. Against thee, thee only, have I sinned, and done this evil in thy sight: that thou mightest be justified when thou speakest, and be clear when thou judgest.

Behold, I was shapen in iniquity; and in sin did my mother conceive me. Behold, thou desirest truth in the inward parts: and in the hidden part thou shalt make me to know wisdom.

Purge me with hyssop, and I shall be clean: wash me, and I shall be whiter than snow. Make me to hear joy and gladness; that the bones which thou hast broken may rejoice. Hide thy face from my sins, and blot out all mine iniquities.

Create in me a clean heart, O God; and renew a right spirit within me. Cast me not away from thy presence; and take not thy holy spirit from me.

Restore unto me the joy of thy salvation; and uphold me with thy free spirit. Then will I teach transgressors thy ways; and sinners shall be converted unto thee.

Deliver me from bloodguiltiness, O God,

thou God of my salvation: and my tongue shall sing aloud of thy righteousness. O Lord, open thou my lips; and my mouth shall shew forth thy praise. For thou desirest not sacrifice; else would I give it: thou delightest not in burnt offering. The sacrifices of God are a broken spirit: a broken and a contrite heart, O God, thou wilt not despise.

Do good in thy good pleasure unto Zion: build thou the walls of Jerusalem. Then shalt thou be pleased with the sacrifices of righteousness, with burnt offering and whole burnt offering: then shall they offer bullocks upon thine altar.

I Talk Back to the Devil

Proclamation #16. Walking in the Fear of the Lord.

> *"Therefore, forsaking the vanity of many, and their false doctrines, let us return to the word which has been handed down to us from the beginning, watching in prayer, persevering in fasting, beseeching in our supplications the all-seeing God not to lead us into temptation."*
>
> – Polycarp

Check this out about the church in the book of Acts.

"Then had the churches rest throughout all Judaea and Galilee and Samaria, and were edified; and walking in the fear of the Lord, and in the comfort of the Holy Ghost, were multiplied."

– Acts 9:31 (KJV)

Some readers are probably thinking … "Uh, yeah. So what?"

Well, here's what's impressive to me about the aforementioned text. The early church was brutally persecuted in every conceivable form and fashion. Including the jailing and the killing of the church's leaders and guess what? The primal church wasn't phased by it.

Nowadays, Christians today lose their minds if they get put in Facebook jail for a week.

Christians today lose their peace if they can't go on vacation every other month.

By the way, here's a question, if you go on vacation and don't post pics of your travels on Instagram, did you really go?

The church today will embrace face masks, lockdowns, and social distancing if some lying Italian doctor tells them to.

I Talk Back to the Devil

The church today doesn't walk in peace, they walk in fear because that's what "The News" is feeding them and they gobble it up and ask for seconds.

If you think I am full of specious doo, take this test. The next time you're around a gaggle of evangelicals, what are they talking about? Are they talking about the end of the world ... fear ... doom and gloom or ... are they talking about kicking demonic butt, saving souls, discipling nations, and the fear of God, not the fear of man?

The early church, in the midst of intense, and oftentimes, deadly persecution had peace, grew strong, were comforted, not terrified, and were empowered by the Holy Spirit and I think it was primarily because they were "walking in the fear of the Lord" and not the fear of man.

The Bible is chock-full of goodies afforded to the believer who walks in the fear of the Lord. For this proclamation, I'm going to plow through the passages in Proverbs and paraphrase and personalize them for you. Are you ready for a mega-dose of the fear of the Lord? You are? Excellent. Let's giddy up.

Shout these out with me ...

THE FEAR OF THE LORD is the beginning of knowledge and only stone-cold fools despise wisdom and instruction. - Proverbs 1:7

THE REASON WHY CALAMITY COMES is because people hate knowledge and did not choose the fear of the Lord. Help me, O God, to always choose the fear of God. - Proverbs 1:29

HELP ME, FATHER, to discern the fear of the Lord and discover the knowledge of God. - Proverbs 2:5

LORD GOD, keep me from being wise in my own eyes; let me live in the fear of the Lord so that I will turn away from evil. The fear of God is good! It will heal my body and refresh my bones. - Proverbs 3:7-8

FILL ME WITH the fear of the Lord, Holy Spirit, so that I will hate evil, pride, arrogance, the evil way, and the perverted mouth. - Proverbs 8:13

LET ME NEVER FORGET, O God, that the fear of the Lord is the beginning of wisdom, and the knowledge of the Holy One is understanding. - Proverbs 9:10

I Talk Back to the Devil

HEAVENLY FATHER, I would like to live a healthy, robust, obedient, Kingdom of God-filled life. Your Word says, "The fear of the Lord prolongs life, but the years of the wicked will be shortened." So please fill me to the brim with the fear of the Lord, Holy Spirit. - Proverbs 10:27

HEAVENLY FATHER, I do not want to be a cowardly Christian chicken with cursed kids. Therefore I choose the fear of the Lord because, according to your Word, in the fear of the Lord there is strong confidence, and my children will have refuge. - Proverbs 14:26

LORD GOD, keep me from fleshly filth and demonic desires. Increase in me the fear of the Lord for it is the true fountain of life that will help me avoid the snares of death. - Proverbs 14:27

IN JESUS'S NAME, I proclaim to myself and every devil in hell that it is better to have little with the fear of the Lord than to have great treasure and turmoil with it.- Proverbs 15:16

I PROCLAIM the fear of the Lord is the true source of wisdom and before God honors me, he first humbles me in his great love. - Proverbs 15:33

THANK YOU, FATHER, for giving me the fear of the Lord because it leads to true life and it gives me the ability to sleep satisfied, untouched by evil. - Proverbs 19:23

I DECLARE your Word, God, that says if I walk in humility and the fear of the Lord, I will be rewarded with riches, honor, and life. - Proverbs 22:4

HOLY SPIRIT, guard my heart against envying sinners and keep me living in the fear of the Lord always. - Proverbs 23:17

LASTLY, FATHER, keep me forever mindful that the fear of man brings a snare … a trap! But he who trusts in the Lord will be exalted. - Proverbs 29:25

HEAVENLY FATHER, thank you for the gift of the fear of the Lord. Keep me walking in a healthy dose of the fear of God, for your glory, in Jesus's name, amen!

I Talk Back to the Devil

Proclamation #17. I Will Have A Godly Marriage.

> *"Our hearts were made for you, Oh Lord, and they are restless until they rest in you."*
>
> – St Augustine

If you want a righteous marriage that doesn't end in disaster do the following …

1. Don't marry an unbeliever. Duh. Or a CINO – a Christian In Name Only. Make certain your spouse has a legit walk with the Lord and isn't a Christian snowflake.

2. Secondly, take marriage seriously. It's easy to get married. It takes work, skill, and a whole lotta grace to stay married.

3. A good place to start working for a God-glorifying marriage is by decreeing this proclamation to heaven and hell, out loud, regarding what you will be and do in your marriage. Remember, life and death are in the power of the tongue – Prov. 18:21.

For the husband, declare ...

HEAVENLY FATHER, help me to defy my flesh, this vapid culture, and all the demons that tempt me to destroy my marriage.

I declare that I'll follow you and you alone with regard to our sacred union.

In Jesus's name, I will love my wife intensely, sacrificially and solely just as Christ loves his bride, the church.

Like Christ, I will give myself up completely for her, provide for her, protect her, and create an atmosphere of righteousness, joy, and peace where she can flourish free from fear. I will respect her and value her as a co-heir in the kingdom of God.

I proclaim that I will afford her a dynamic place where she can be alive to God and his eternal purpose. This is my responsibility and I embrace it fully knowing that if I do not fulfill this duty that I am denying the faith and I'm worse than an unbeliever.

I will not be an absent husband or a flippant man, who abuses and abandons his wife. Therefore, I proclaim that I'll care for my wife as if my very life was on the line.

This is what God calls a godly union. This is what God ordains, blesses, and joins together. Everything else is earthly and demonic.

Keep my heart in the scriptures, O God, regarding my headship and my solemn role in my marriage.

Lord God, I proclaim that I will be a good husband and honor my wife and delight in her. I understand if I don't, that according to 1 Peter 3:8, you will turn a deaf ear to all of my prayer requests.

I proclaim that I'll love and protect my wife as if she was my heart and soul. In Jesus's name, amen.

For the wife, proclaim …

LORD, I declare my support and understanding for my godly husband who's providing righteous leadership in our marriage the way Christ does to his church.

Just as the church submits to Jesus, as he provides such holy leadership, so I will likewise submit to my husband as he follows God's lead for our life.

I proclaim I will not become a contentious woman. I will not become a selfish mother. I will help create a kingdom home of righteousness, peace, and joy in the Holy Ghost. In Jesus's name, amen!

I Talk Back to the Devil

Proclamation #18. I Will Imitate God.

"The secret of success in Christ's Kingdom is the ability to pray."

– E. M. Bounds

If you'd like to live a God-honoring, politically incorrect lifestyle, then I recommend asking God for a major Holy Spirit infusion of Ephesians 5:1-20. One thing is for certain, if you follow the edicts found here in Paul's letter to the Ephesians, family reunions will never be boring.

Doug Giles

"Be ye therefore followers of God, as dear children; And walk in love, as Christ also hath loved us, and hath given himself for us an offering and a sacrifice to God for a sweetsmelling savour. But fornication, and all uncleanness, or covetousness, let it not be once named among you, as becometh saints; Neither filthiness, nor foolish talking, nor jesting, which are not convenient: but rather giving of thanks. For this ye know, that no whoremonger, nor unclean person, nor covetous man, who is an idolater, hath any inheritance in the kingdom of Christ and of God. Let no man deceive you with vain words: for because of these things cometh the wrath of God upon the children of disobedience. Be not ye therefore partakers with them. For ye were sometimes darkness, but now are ye light in the Lord: walk as children of light: (For the fruit of the Spirit is in all goodness and righteousness and truth;) Proving what is acceptable unto the Lord. And have no fellowship with the unfruitful works of darkness, but rather reprove them. For it is a shame even to speak of those things which are done of them in secret. But all things that are reproved are made

I Talk Back to the Devil

manifest by the light: for whatsoever doth make manifest is light. Wherefore he saith, Awake thou that sleepest, and arise from the dead, and Christ shall give thee light. See then that ye walk circumspectly, not as fools, but as wise, Redeeming the time, because the days are evil. Wherefore be ye not unwise, but understanding what the will of the Lord is. And be not drunk with wine, wherein is excess; but be filled with the Spirit; Speaking to yourselves in psalms and hymns and spiritual songs, singing and making melody in your heart to the Lord; Giving thanks always for all things unto God and the Father in the name of our Lord Jesus Christ."

– Eph. 5:1-20 (KJV)

Here's my prayer from that text paraphrased and personalized for you. Now, it's up to you to declare this, in faith, at the devil, before your buddies, and ultimately, before the throne of God. Enjoy …

HOLY SPIRIT help me to imitate God.

I proclaim that I will keep company with Jesus and learn to love the way he does.

Jesus didn't dole out his love sparingly but abundantly. He didn't do it to get something from us but to give everything of himself to us and Lord, I want to love like that.

Keep me, O God, from sexual promiscuity, dirty deeds, and a heart filled with greed.

Heavenly Father, make me hate the taste of gossip, dirty talk, and stupid silly nonsense and make thanksgiving and praise my go-to mode of speech.

Dear God, let me never use people or Christianity, as an avenue to advance my selfish gain as that has nothing to do with the kingdom of God.

Father, make me to be shrewd as a serpent and not to be taken in by religious smooth talk from people who are far away from you. That garbage ticks you off. I declare that I won't hang around those religious hucksters.

I declare, by your grace, O God, that I will pursue the good, the right, and the true. I will, by your power, stay away from the darkness and will figure out what pleases you and I will do that.

I will not waste my time on vanity and the empty pursuits of darkness, but will rather expose such things for the demonic schemes that they are.

Lord God Almighty, help me to watch my step, use my head, and make the most out of every opportunity that comes my way for your kingdom concerns.

I will not live carelessly and unthinkingly but will seek to understand what you want, O Lord.

If I drink, I will not get drunk. If I do get drunk, it'll be on the Holy Spirit of which I will drink huge drafts of his intoxicating influence.

Make me, O God, a holy loudmouth filled with your praise, constantly singing the psalms, and making any excuse possible to praise your holy name.

In Jesus's name, amen!

Proclamation #19. Make Me An Acts 2:42 Christian, Lord!

"Prayer is the link that connects us with God."

– A.B. Simpson

"They were continually devoting themselves to the apostles' teaching and to fellowship, to the breaking of bread and to prayer."

– Acts 2:42

I don't know about you but I never wanted to make the body of Christ, i.e., the church, suffer because I was some dilatory spiritual toad. That's been my ambition ever since I got converted way back in 1983. Now, as you can imagine, I have failed multiple times at that noble goal. However, by God's grace, I've repented and have run hard towards God's high calling for *mi vida* versus languishing in a sad and lackluster slough of evangelical despond.

One of the scriptures that kicks my backside back into Holy Ghost gear when I need it is the aforementioned text I touched off this proclamation with namely … "They were continually devoting themselves to the apostles' teaching and to fellowship, to the breaking of bread and to prayer." – Acts 2:42

Dr. Luke notes four particulars that the early church sported in spades that were the ground bed for true biblical growth, massive cultural impact, and for the toppling of many kings and kingdoms. Check out how these Christians operated …

1. They were continually devoting themselves to the apostles' teaching.

2. They were continually devoting themselves to fellowship.

3. They were continually devoting themselves to the breaking of bread.

4. They were continually devoting themselves to prayer.

With those four simple things the church, under massive persecution and with no mega marketing budget, or big screens, skinny jeans, and smoke machines, exploded with growth in a very anti-Christian environment. Imagine that.

I think we should get biblical and kick it old school again in relation to what we as Christians should be and may be. Oh, and maybe we will see the fruit the primal church beheld in the book of Acts.

Proclaim that this is the kind of believer you're going to be!

HEAVENLY FATHER, give me a deep hunger for the apostle's doctrine. Give me a deep desire for scripture. Make me long for the pure milk of the Word. Make the Word of God more precious than silver to me and more costly than gold. I proclaim the scripture shall be my meditation 24/7/365. Indeed, I will be continually devoting myself to the apostles' teaching and not what this crass culture has to offer. I will renew my mind according to your holy Word.

In addition, Lord, make me a devotee to true biblical fellowship. Where iron sharpens iron. Where covenant relationships flourish and accountability and encouragement thrive and take root. Establish me with like-minded warriors. Plant me in the house of God. Let me not be some sketchy tumbleweed Christian who floats from church to church or completely ignores the regular gathering of believers which is stupid and spiritually dangerous.

Lord, I declare I want to be, by your power and might, faithful to your communion table, partaking in the Bread of Life, with other believers who are serious about leaving a big scar on Satan's backside. The Lord's Supper will be something that I long for and celebrate, for it memorializes the Lord's sacrifice for his people. He became sin for us so that we can become righteous before him. That's quite the exchange, and God help me to never take communion lightly but enjoy it often and thoroughly.

And lastly, Lord, make me a praying maniac. Completely devoted to coming boldly before your throne of grace. Praying about anything and

I Talk Back to the Devil

everything. Speaking to my mountains. Wielding the sword of the Spirit in intercession against principalities and powers. Make prayer the first and last thing I do, O God. Holy Spirit teach me how to pray like Jesus, Moses, David, Paul, and all the other great men and women who shook all of hell when they let fly with their prayers. Help me, Holy Spirit, to be that kind of believer that continually devotes themselves to the apostles' teaching, and to fellowship, to the breaking of bread, and to prayer." In Jesus's name, amen!

Proclamation #20. I Will Be A Generous and Cheerful Giver.

> *"The entire day receives order and discipline when it acquires unity. This unity must be sought and found in morning prayer. The morning prayer determines the day."*
>
> – Dietrich Bonhoeffer

This next proclamation will drive the miserly and greedy religious person mad because it's all about being a cheerful giver who loves blessing God's people doing God's work.

HOLY SPIRIT, make me remember, with regard to my financial giving, that if I'm a stingy planter I will get a tiny crop, and if I'm a big planter I will get a huge crop.

Crucify in me, O God, the love of money that doesn't give or only begrudgingly gives. I want to be a giver who loves giving and doesn't need my arm twisted or told a sad story before I'll give anything.

Your Word declares, O God, that You will pour out your blessings in amazing ways so that I am financially ready for anything life tosses at me.

You, Lord, are most generous with me and you supply my financial needs so that I can be generous in all kinds of ways that bless other people. I thank you, Father, for providing for me and inspiring me to be a blessing to others with what you have blessed me, in Jesus's name, amen!

Here's the biblical backdrop for that last proclamation …

> "Now this I say, he who sows sparingly will also reap sparingly, and he who sows bountifully will also reap bountifully. Each one must do just as he has purposed in his

heart, not grudgingly or under compulsion, for God loves a cheerful giver. And God is able to make all grace abound to you, so that always having all sufficiency in everything, you may have an abundance for every good deed; as it is written,

> 'He scattered abroad, he gave to the poor,
> His righteousness endures forever.'"

Now he who supplies seed to the sower and bread for food will supply and multiply your seed for sowing and increase the harvest of your righteousness; you will be enriched in everything for all liberality, which through us is producing thanksgiving to God."

– 2 Corinthians 9:6-11 (NASB)

Our Warfare in Christ.

Proclamation #21. I Will Not Live in Fear.

> *"Rough, boisterous, stormy and altogether warlike, I am born to fight against innumerable monsters and devils."*
>
> – Martin Luther

If you've been caught up in the world's mass delusional psychosis and you're worried about your health, your job, our nation and your kid's future; shout these bad boys at the devil and his defeated ilk. The following verses have been personalized and paraphrased by yours truly. Pray aloud, with oomph, and declare them often.

I PROCLAIM in the mighty name of Jesus that God has not called me to be a fear-laden hamster. God has given me power, love, and a sound, rational, biblical mind. – 2Tim.1:7.

I PROCLAIM in the mighty name of Jesus that God will not allow any weapon that is formed against me to prosper. And every smack-talking yapping demon that comes against me in judgment, God will smash them with his mighty power. This is my birthright. This is what I can confidently expect my God will do for me when demons and the people they control attempt to take me down. – Isa.54:17

I PROCLAIM in the mighty name of Jesus that, by God's grace and strength, I will not be afraid if tens of thousands of people or tens of thousands of demons set themselves against me round about. I can be confident because God will arise and save me. Not only will he rescue my backside but he'll also smash all my enemy's cheekbones and smash their teeth out. Salvation, protection, and God's blessing will be upon me, in Jesus's mighty name. – Ps. 3.6-8

I PROCLAIM in the mighty name of Jesus that I live in the shelter of the Most High God and

I Talk Back to the Devil

I rest under the shadow of the Almighty. This I declare about the Lord: He alone is my refuge, my place of safety; he is my God, and I trust him. For he will rescue me from every trap, forgive every sin, and protect me from deadly disease. – Ps. 91:1-3

I PROCLAIM in the mighty name of Jesus that I am not going to worry about anything but instead, pray about everything. I'm going to tell God what I need, and thank him for all that he has done for me and fear can go pound sand. – Phil. 4:6

I PROCLAIM in the mighty name of Jesus that I will cast all my anxieties upon him because he cares for me. – 1Peter 5:7

Proclamation #22. Jesus Rules and Satan Drools.

> *"The Prince of the power of the air seems to bend all the force of his attack against the spirit of prayer."*
>
> – Andrew Bonar

It's wild how many Christian, consciously or unconsciously, think Satan rules this world and Jesus only reigns in heaven in some kind of mystical/spiritual sense of the word.

Yep, listening to most evangelical doom-n-gloomers talk about what's going down on this *terra firma*, one walks away with the strong notion that they believe in a big Antichrist and little Jesus Christ.

Indeed, for them, Satan wins in time and Jesus wins in eternity and any belief to the contrary to their sad eschatology of defeat is the equivalent of polishing brass on a sinking ship. The biblical prophets didn't see Jesus's incarnation as powerless and uneventful. For instance, check out what Isaiah said of Jesus and what would occur after his first coming …

> "For a child will be born to us, a son will be given to us; And the government will rest on His shoulders; And His name will be called Wonderful Counselor, Mighty God, Eternal Father, Prince of Peace. There will be no end to the increase of His government or of peace, on the throne of David and over his kingdom, to establish it and to uphold it with justice and righteousness from then on and forevermore. The zeal of the Lord of hosts will accomplish this."
>
> – Isaiah 9:6-7 (NASB)"

I Talk Back to the Devil

Allow me to turn that text into a proclamation of Jesus's rule and reign and not the devil's. Pull this prayer out when gloomy Christians start talking about how bad it's getting and how powerful evil men and women are running roughshod over God's people, his Word and his works. Maybe this'll talk them off the ledge and give them a mega dose of biblical hope.

Y'all ready? Belt this one out with me. Say with me in a loud voice …

HEAVENLY FATHER, you are my Rock, my Strong Tower, and the Defense of My Life.

I declare in the mighty name of Jesus that at Christ's first coming – not his second coming – through his death, burial, resurrection, and ascension, that he, and he alone, has all authority in heaven and on earth. Period.

I declare what Isaiah prophesied – that Jesus rules the world and all government rests on his shoulders.

This power does not belong to the devil, or some crooked politician, or an ideology held sacred by a group of whack-jobs trying to hijack our planet for their wicked desires.

I proclaim that Jesus' ruling power will grow, in time, on the earth, through the church and it will not shrink, and everywhere it goes it will bring peace and wholeness.

I declare that Christ will establish a heavenly kingdom on the earth that is rock-solid, firm, and steadfast. That kingdom will establish biblical justice and righteousness on the earth and will wipe out Satan's demonic desires.

This epic rule and reign of Jesus is not put off until his second coming, but it has been going on ever since his incarnation and will aggressively continue forevermore through his spirit-filled church.

And we know his good works and his rule and reign will not fail because the zeal of God of the Angel Armies will drive it on wiping out Satan's habitations with glorious devastations. In Jesus's mighty name, amen!

I Talk Back to the Devil

Proclamation #23. Adios, Evil Leaders.

> *"If you are strangers to prayer you are strangers to power."*
>
> – Billy Sunday

A lot of people, for many, many serious reasons, are wringing their hands nowadays over the glide path our nation is tooling down thanks to the Marxist morons inside the Beltway.

Yep, at this writing, our current bevy of "leaders" care for that which is holy, just, and good about as much as a badger cares what a prairie dog feels when he's chewing on his carotid artery.

I've personally seen and heard many Christians buy into this hand wringing over the state of our union, and I have wondered aloud, "Why don't you, dear Christian, cease to sweat these godless leaders and pray that God either convert them or sort them out?"

In Psalm 2, David's not sweating a culture's smack talking against God. He's not curled up in the fetal position, sucking his thumb, and wetting his pants over their godless and goofy plots to be free of God and cut loose from his law.

Matter of fact, David's reaction is just the opposite of what most sad Christians are boo-hooing about during these days of declension.

Indeed, David states that when rebel-kings start smack-talking God and attempt to dispense with his decrees that God mocks them. Yep, Jehovah's amused at these presumptive idiots who wish to lead a nation without giving God honor by adhering to his way.

And he doesn't just laugh, as you're about to see, he gets ticked off and that's bad news bears for the fools attempting to cast loose from God's gracious moorings.

Ergo, dear Christian, instead of chewing your

I Talk Back to the Devil

fingernails down to the nub and buying the fear that saddles the faithless, why don't you pray out loud Psalm 2 that David prayed and penned many moons ago?

Here's the actual Psalm …

> Why do the heathen rage, and the people imagine a vain thing? The kings of the earth set themselves, and the rulers take counsel together, against the Lord, and against his anointed, saying, Let us break their bands asunder, and cast away their cords from us.
>
> He that sitteth in the heavens shall laugh: the Lord shall have them in derision. Then shall he speak unto them in his wrath, and vex them in his sore displeasure. Yet have I set my king upon my holy hill of Zion.
>
> I will declare the decree: the Lord hath said unto me, Thou art my Son; this day have I begot- ten thee. Ask of me, and I shall give thee the heathen for thine inheritance, and the uttermost parts of the earth for thy possession. Thou shalt break them with a rod of iron; thou shalt dash them in pieces like a potter's vessel.
>
> – Ps. 2:1-9 (KJV)

Doug Giles

Here's our proclamation …

LORD, WE DECLARE, according to your Word, that leaders and nations, who rage against that which is holy, just, and good, and try to outwit you are veritable fools and not political geniuses. Indeed, their days are numbered.

Every summit conference that they hold, with their dipstick plots against our Lord Jesus and his glorious decrees, God Almighty mocks and laughs at and finds them highly amusing because they are so ridiculously stupid and foolish.

We declare that not only does God ridicule their puny plans, he also will rebuke them in his fierce fury and will fill them with holy fear, terrifying them in his wrath.

Indeed, God will remove evil leaders and replace them with leaders who love his law.

We declare that according to the Word of God, the Son of God rules the world. The nations belong to him and not the Devil and some pathetic antichrist.

I Talk Back to the Devil

Speaking of the Devil and his ilk, Jesus will smash them and their evil dreams with a rod of iron. Jesus will dash them like a clay pot, in Jesus's name, amen!

Proclamation #24. God Dooms the Great Men of the World.

> *"Prayer lays hold of God's plan and becomes the link between his will and its accomplishment on earth. Amazing things happen, and we are given the privilege of being the channels of the Holy Spirit's prayer."*
>
> – Elisabeth Elliot

"Are you so ignorant? Are you so deaf to the words of God—the words he gave before the world began? Have you never heard nor understood? It is God who sits above the circle of the earth. (The people below must seem to him like grasshoppers!) he is the one who stretches out the heavens like a curtain and makes his tent from them. He dooms the great men of the world and brings them all to naught. They hardly get started, barely take root, when he blows on them and their work withers, and the wind carries them off like straw. "With whom will you compare me? Who is my equal?" asks the Holy One. Look up into the heavens! Who created all these stars? As a shepherd leads his sheep, calling each by its pet name, and counts them to see that none are lost or strayed, so God does with stars and planets! O Jacob, O Israel, how can you say that the Lord doesn't see your troubles and isn't being fair? Don't you yet understand? Don't you know by now that the everlasting God, the Creator of the farthest parts of the earth, never grows faint or weary? No one can fathom the depths of his understanding. He gives power to the tired and worn out, and strength to the weak. Even the youths shall be exhausted, and the young men will all give up. But they that wait upon the Lord shall renew their strength. They shall mount

I Talk Back to the Devil

up with wings like eagles; they shall run and not be weary; they shall walk and not faint."

– Isa.40:21-31 (TLB)

Wow. What a powerful block of scripture. Isaiah sure wasn't buffaloed into believing that evil men were going to hijack God's planet and dispense with his rule. On the contrary, Isaiah says, "He dooms the great men of the world and brings them all to naught. They hardly get started, barely take root, when he blows on them and their work withers, and the wind carries them off like straw (Isa.40:23-24)". You rarely hear evangelicals talking that way when they describe the poo-poo *el grande* our nation and this third rock from the sun is facing. These weenies make the devil and evil men seem bigger than God, and that there's no way their evil machinations can be stopped, and the church's only hope is the rapture. Isaiah didn't roll like that.

Succinctly, Isaiah said that God is about to whoop some evil backside in grand fashion. That's what he declared and that's what we should declare.

Proclaim this with me, out loud, with testicular fortitude.

FATHER, WE DECLARE, in the mighty name of Jesus, it is you who sits above the circle of the earth, not some powerful evil man, woman, group, or wicked nation.

We agree with your word, that these so-called mighty, evil mongers are mere grasshoppers to you and that they are doomed and you will bring them to naught.

We declare their evil plans will not take root and that you will blow away their works and carry their garbage off like a tornado does to a mobile home.

Nobody compares to you, Oh Lord. No one is your equal.

We declare, O Lord, that you see our trouble and that you're not too busy, nor too weary, nor too faint to come to our rescue.

When we get tired or worn out with the enemy's garbage, as individuals and as a nation, we declare that you will give renewed strength to the weak, and that we will mount up with wings like eagles, and that we shall run and not grow weary

I Talk Back to the Devil

… walk and not faint … all because we cried out to you, and we waited on you, and our cry for help did not land on deaf ears, in Jesus's name, amen!

Proclamation #25. We Are More Than Conquerors.

> *"We are to pray in times of adversity, lest we become faithless and unbelieving. We are to pray in times of prosperity, lest we become boastful and proud. We are to pray in times of danger, lest we become fearful and doubting. We are to pray in times of security, lest we become self-sufficient."*
>
> – Billy Graham

Because of God's great love toward us he's not going to allow demons, or our flesh, or our enemies, both physical and spiritual, or any weapon hell wields our way to clean our clock.

In addition, we were not born again to barely get by but rather we overwhelmingly conquer via the power of the Holy Spirit. Romans 8:31-39 spells that fact out in unmistakable fashion, and I have paraphrased that passage for our next proclamation.

Are you ready to declare your victory? If you said yes, then giddy up and shout this one at the powers of darkness.

Here we go …

IN THE GREAT, AWESOME, AND EPIC NAME OF JESUS, by his power and doing, I proclaim that God is on my side, and, therefore, I have nothing to fear from men or devils.

If God did not spare his own Son but handed him over on my account then he will definitely and graciously give me all things.

No matter what men or devils say, God has chosen me and declared me, "not guilty".

No one has the authority to condemn me.

I Talk Back to the Devil

Jesus Christ, who died and rose again, sits at the right hand of God where he pleads my case on my behalf.

Nothing and no one can separate me from God.

Nothing can come between God's love for me.

Troubles cannot separate me from Jesus.

Hardships cannot separate me from Jesus.

Persecution cannot separate me from Jesus.

Hunger cannot separate me from Jesus.

Poverty cannot separate me from Jesus.

Danger cannot separate me from Jesus.

Death cannot separate me from Jesus.

No matter what life and the devil may bring to me, I will always taste victory through Jesus because of his great love for me.

In the name of Jesus, I have every confidence that nothing – not death, life, angels, demons, the present, the future, spiritual forces of wickedness, nor any created being can come between me and God's love for me as revealed in Jesus my Lord, amen!

Here's how King Jimmy put it …

Doug Giles

"What shall we then say to these things? If God be for us, who can be against us? He that spared not his own Son, but delivered him up for us all, how shall he not with him also freely give us all things? Who shall lay anything to the charge of God's elect? It is God that justifieth. Who is he that condemneth? It is Christ that died, yea rather, that is risen again, who is even at the right hand of God, who also maketh intercession for us. Who shall separate us from the love of Christ? shall tribulation, or distress, or persecution, or famine, or nakedness, or peril, or sword? As it is written, For thy sake we are killed all the day long; we are accounted as sheep for the slaughter. Nay, in all these things we are more than conquerors through him that loved us. For I am persuaded, that neither death, nor life, nor angels, nor principalities, nor powers, nor things present, nor things to come, Nor height, nor depth, nor any other creature, shall be able to separate us from the love of God, which is in Christ Jesus our Lord."

– Romans 8:31-39 (KJV)

I Talk Back to the Devil

Proclamation #26. Old and Dangerous.

> *"If you believe in prayer at all, expect God to hear you. If you do not expect, you will not have. God will not hear you unless you believe He will hear you; but if you believe He will, He will be as good as your faith."*
>
> – Charles Spurgeon

"In thee, O Lord, do I put my trust: let me never be put to confusion. Deliver me in thy righteousness, and cause me to escape: incline thine ear unto me, and save me. Be thou my strong habitation, whereunto I may continually resort: thou hast given commandment to save me; for thou art my rock and my fortress.

Deliver me, O my God, out of the hand of the wicked, out of the hand of the unrighteous and cruel man. For thou art my hope, O Lord God: thou art my trust from my youth. By thee have I been holden up from the womb: thou art he that took me out of my mother's bowels: my praise shall be continually of thee.

I am as a wonder unto many; but thou art my strong refuge. Let my mouth be filled with thy praise and with thy honour all the day.

Cast me not off in the time of old age; forsake me not when my strength faileth. For mine enemies speak against me; and they that lay wait for my soul take counsel together, Saying, God hath forsaken him: persecute and take him; for there is none to deliver him.

O God, be not far from me: O my God, make haste for my help. Let them be confounded and consumed that are adversaries to my soul; let them be covered with reproach and dishonour that seek my hurt.

I Talk Back to the Devil

But I will hope continually, and will yet praise thee more and more. My mouth shall shew forth thy righteousness and thy salvation all the day; for I know not the numbers thereof. I will go in the strength of the Lord God: I will make mention of thy righteousness, even of thine only.

O God, thou hast taught me from my youth: and hitherto have I declared thy wondrous works. Now also when I am old and greyheaded, O God, forsake me not; until I have shewed thy strength unto this generation, and thy power to every one that is to come.

Thy righteousness also, O God, is very high, who hast done great things: O God, who is like unto thee! Thou, which hast shewed me great and sore troubles, shalt quicken me again, and shalt bring me up again from the depths of the earth. Thou shalt increase my greatness, and comfort me on every side.

I will also praise thee with the psaltery, even thy truth, O my God: unto thee will I sing with the harp, O thou Holy One of Israel. My lips shall greatly rejoice when I sing unto thee; and my soul, which thou hast redeemed. My tongue also shall talk of thy righteousness all the day long: for they are confounded, for they are brought unto shame, that seek my hurt."

– Ps. 71 (KJV)

In Psalm seventy-one David's under duress and he's old now. It doesn't say what David did, but he's still ticking off all the right people and he's a senior citizen.

The psalmist says he's under the threat of humiliation and disgrace. His enemies have cornered him. Sinful people, unjust and cruel, were after him. His enemies are voicing evil against him. Can you feel this?

His adversaries are plotting his demise in secret.

Here's an interesting little ditty they probably never told you at youth group. A ton of David's opposition came from the supposed "people of God" and not just the Philistines. Anyhoo ... I digress.

David's enemies are walking around yapping that God's abandoned David and it's time to seize him because no one will come to his rescue.

I Talk Back to the Devil

David has seen hard times ... many miserable days ... and now he says he's found himself in a pit. I don't know if this is a literal pit or a metaphorical pit but whatever it is ... it sucks.

So, how would you respond if you were David? Shoot heroin? Drink a big bottle of vodka? Mainline PeptoBismol? Renounce your faith, become a raging atheist, and join a Marilyn Manson cover band?

David didn't say, "I quit."

Oh. Heck. No.

Here's what David did when getting jackhammered by his various enemies when he's old and gray. I've paraphrased these passages and personalized them for you to proclaim when all of hell comes against you because you're still a threat to the enemy. Are you ready? You are? Well, let's roll.

Remember to belt these bad boys out loud.

LORD, I DECLARE, in the mighty name of Jesus, you are my shelter and you'll protect me from all humiliation and disgrace.

When the enemy comes against me you'll turn your ear to me and rescue me, save me, and deliver me from all my enemies.

I declare, in the mighty name of Jesus, that you are my Rock, my Fortress, my Solid Ground, and that you keep me safe.

When evil men and devils assail me, O God, you will deliver me from the power of sinful, unjust, and cruel men.

You are my hope, O Lord. I have trusted you since I was young. I will sing your praises and proclaim your power all day long.

Thank you, Lord, for not setting me aside now when I am old and when my dumb enemies think that you have dumped me and that I am worn out, and of no use.

Lord God, cover these devils with shame. Pulverize them with contempt and disgrace.

If the enemy wants me to shut up and despair, I will do the opposite by keeping hope alive and increasing my praise and worship of you ten-fold.

Yes, Lord … if they want to shut me up I will increase my telling of your merciful acts. I will tell everyone about how you deliver through your great power and how holy and just you are.

I Talk Back to the Devil

Holy Spirit, where the enemy has tried to shut me down, I ask you as my hair turns gray, that you not only not abandon me, but give me a fresh vision and mission to talk about your power and strength to the next generation.

Father, I proclaim, that even though I've seen hard times, and, I've experienced some truly horrible days, you will restore me again and raise me up from the pit. Not only that, but you will greatly increase my status and comfort me much to the chagrin of devils and evil men.

I thank you for your faithfulness. I will shout for joy because of you. I will sing your praises and will celebrate your powerful saving grace. All day long I will proclaim how you hammered those who plotted to bring me harm, and now they're the ones who are ashamed and humiliated, in Jesus's name, amen!

Share this proclamation with your feisty granddad or grandmother.

Proclamation #27. Peace in the Storm.

> *"Prayer does not change God, but it changes him who prays. "*
>
> — Soren Kierkegaard

If you've been plagued by fear and you're worried about your health, your job, our nation, the church, and your kid's future; shout these bad boys at the devil and his defeated ilk …

FOR GOD hath not given me a spirit of fear; but of power, and of love, and of a sound mind. – 2Tim. 1:7 (KJV)

NO WEAPON that is formed against me shall prosper; and every tongue that shall rise against me in judgment thou shalt condemn. This is the heritage of the servants of the Lord, and their righteousness is of me, saith the Lord. – Isa. 54:17 (KJV)

WHAT TIME I AM AFRAID, I will trust in thee. In God I will praise his word, in God I have put my trust; I will not fear what flesh can do unto me. – Ps. 56:3-4 (KJV)

I WILL NOT BE AFRAID of ten thousands of people that have set themselves against me round about. Arise, O Lord; save me, O my God: for thou hast smitten all mine enemies upon the cheek bone; thou hast broken the teeth of the ungodly. Salvation belongeth unto the Lord: Thy blessing is upon Thy people. – Ps. 3.6-8 (KJV)

THOSE WHO LIVE IN THE SHELTER OF THE MOST HIGH will find rest in the shadow of the Almighty. This I declare about the Lord: he alone is my refuge, my place of safety; he is my God, and I trust him. For he will rescue me from every trap and protect me from deadly disease.– Ps. 91:1-3 (KJV)

I'M NOT GOING TO WORRY ABOUT ANYTHING; instead, I'll pray about everything. I will tell God what I need and thank him for all he has done. – Phil. 4:6

Or as The Message translation puts it in verses six and seven, "… [I WILL NOT] fret or worry. Instead of worrying, [I will] pray. [I will let] petitions and praises shape [my] worries into prayers, letting God know [my] concerns. Before [I] know it, a sense of God's wholeness, everything coming together for good, will come and settle [me] down. It's wonderful what happens when Christ displaces worry at the center of [my] life."

I WILL CAST all my anxiety on him because he cares about me. – 1 Pet. 5:7 (NASB).

Here's the Phillips translation … [I WILL] throw the whole weight of my anxieties upon him, for [I am] his personal concern.

THESE THINGS I have spoken to you, so that in Me you may have peace. In the world you have tribulation, but take courage; I have overcome the world. – John 16:33 (NASB)

THE LORD IS GOOD, a stronghold in the day of trouble, and He knows those who take refuge in Him. – Nah. 1:7 (NASB).

DON'T WORRY about anything; instead, pray about everything. Tell God what you need, and thank him for all he has done. – Phil. 4:6 (NLT)

WHAT SHALL I SAY about such wonderful things as these? If God is for me, who can ever be against me? – Rom. 8:31 (NLT)

THE FAITHFUL LOVE of the Lord never ends! His mercies never cease. Great is his faithfulness; his mercies begin afresh each morning. – Lam. 3:22-23 (NLT)

I AM GOD'S MASTERPIECE. He has created me anew in Christ Jesus, so I can do the good things he planned for me long ago. – Eph. 2:10 (NLT)

I Talk Back to the Devil

BOLDLY CONFESSING and obeying his Word is how we "resist the devil" causing him to flee from us and our land! – 1 Pet. 5:8,9

Proclamation #28. All Authority Belongs to Jesus.

> *"A fiery shield is God's Word; of more substance and purer than gold, which, tried in the fire, loses nought of its substance, but resists and overcomes all the fury of the fiery heat; even so, he that believes God's Word overcomes all, and remains secure everlastingly, against all misfortunes; for this shield fears nothing, neither hell nor the devil."*
>
> – Martin Luther

A lot of Christians think Satan's running the planet and the end of the world is just around the corner. Yep ... the unspoken/spoken message via evangelicalism is that Satan wins in time and Jesus wins in eternity.

I'm about to contradict all that nonsense with what the scripture states about who's running this third rock from the sun. Declare the following, out loud, with holy boldness.

FATHER I DECLARE your Word that says all authority in heaven and on earth has been given to Jesus and not to the devil (Mt.28:18). Christ alone has all authority. And it is not just in heaven, but it's also here on the earth!

ALL THINGS have been handed over to Jesus by his heavenly Father. – Mt.11:27

THE FATHER LOVES the Son and has given all things into his hand. – Jn.3:35

GOD RAISED JESUS from the dead and seated him at his right hand in the heavenly places, far above all rule and authority and power and dominion, and above every name that is named, not only in this age but also in the one to come. – Eph.1:20-21

I Talk Back to the Devil

FATHER, you have and you will glorify your Son that the Son may glorify you, since you have given him authority over all flesh, to give eternal life to all whom you have given him. – Jn.17:2

LORD GOD we proclaim your Word which states that Jesus sustains the world — he is the radiance of the glory of God and the exact imprint of his nature, and he upholds the universe by the word of his power. – Heb.1:3

JESUS IS before all things, and in him all things hold together. – Col. 1:17

WE DECLARE that Christ and Christ alone governs all of nature. From the wildflowers to the little sparrows to a West Texas F5 tornado, Christ rules them all. It is Jesus who commands even the wind and the water, and they obey him. (Luke 8:25). The entire creative order is under his control.

LORD GOD, I declare your Word which states Jesus's complete authority over Satan and all his demons. The devil and all unclean spirits must obey him (Mark 1:27) and Satan cannot touch the children of God without permission. – 1 Jn 5:18

OUR MIGHTY JESUS rules and oversees all of history. When evil leaders "Make war on the

Lamb ... the Lamb will conquer them, for he is Lord of lords and King of kings, and those with him are called and chosen and faithful." – Revelation 17:14

THE BOOK OF DANIEL SAYS, "[God] removes kings and sets up kings; ... the Most High rules the kingdom of men and gives it to whom he will ... he does according to his will among the host of heaven and among the inhabitants of the earth; and none can stay his hand or say to him, 'What have you done?'" – Daniel 2:21; 4:17, 35 (ESV)

INDEED, Psalm 2 says God laughs, mocks, ridicules, and harshly judges rulers who set their heart against him and his Word. Lord, I declare that every decision made by every wicked ruler against the church and mission of Christ will, in time, backfire spectacularly in their face, in Jesus's name, amen. – Isa.54:16,17

LORD, we proclaim that Jesus has authority over all sicknesses and diseases.

LORD, we declare that Jesus has not lost any of his power to heal between today and the first century when "He went about doing good and healing all who were oppressed by the devil, for God was with Him."– Acts 10:38 (ESV)

I Talk Back to the Devil

LORD, we proclaim that Jesus can lift any disease he pleases at any time he pleases.

NEITHER SATAN, nor COVID, nor viruses, nor bacteria, nor spike proteins are sovereign in this world. Jesus is. No disease will stop his mission.

HEAVENLY FATHER, I declare that by Jesus's death he might broke the power of him who holds the power of death – that is, the devil (Heb.2:14) and we longer have to fear death because of your great love and sacrifice for us.

JESUS RULES over my death. Which means nothing can separate me from the love of Christ. Shall tribulation, or distress, or persecution, or famine, or nakedness, or danger, or sword? As it is written, "For your sake we are being killed all day long; we are regarded as sheep to be slaughtered." No, in all these things we are more than conquerors through him who loved us. – Romans 8:35–37 (ESV)

YOUR WORD DECLARES, "Death is swallowed up in victory." "O death, where is your victory? O death, where is your sting?" I am not afraid of death. I fear only God and not what mortal man can do to me.

LORD GOD, I proclaim what Jesus said when he decreed "I will build My church, and the gates of hell shall not prevail against it" (– Matthew 16:18 ESV). He will not fail. His mission will not fail. His church will not fail. Nothing of his eternal purpose will be thwarted. As your Word says …

> "I am God, and there is no other;
> I am God, and there is none like me,
> declaring the end from the beginning
> and from ancient times things not yet done,
> saying, "My counsel shall stand,
> and I will accomplish all my purpose."
>
> – Isaiah 46:9–10 (ESV)

FATHER, we stand in faith proclaiming, with holy boldness, the rule and reign of Jesus Christ over all of the world, in Christ's name, amen!

I Talk Back to the Devil

Proclamation #29. Speak to Your Mountain.

"Pray, and let God worry."

– Martin Luther

If you have raging obstacles confronting you that seem insurmountable then this biblical proclamation is for you! It comes straight from our Savior's mouth in Mark 11:22-26. Are you ready? Let's roll.

LORD GOD, I declare my trust in you and your love for me.

Since I have great trust in you, I say to every mountain, every difficulty, every satanic hindrance, all interferences by wicked men, to uproot yourself and throw yourself into the sea and out of my life and out of my way.

I declare I do not doubt, but indeed I trust that what I say will take place, it will come to pass and it will happen.

I proclaim the promise that Jesus made to me that whatever I pray for or ask from God I believe that I will receive it and I will.

And Lord God, I forgive all those who have wronged me. I will not live in bitterness and in spite. I release them and forgive them in Jesus's name, amen.

Thank you and praise you, Jesus for ripping mountains out of my life and making a way where there is no way.

Here's the passage this proclamation was crafted from.

> "And Jesus answered saying to them, "Have faith in God. Truly I say to you, whoever says to this mountain, 'Be taken up and cast into the sea,' and does not doubt in his heart, but believes that what he says is

I Talk Back to the Devil

going to happen, it will be *granted* him. Therefore I say to you, all things for which you pray and ask, believe that you have received them, and they will be *granted* you. Whenever you stand praying, forgive, if you have anything against anyone, so that your Father who is in heaven will also forgive you your transgressions. But if you do not forgive, neither will your Father who is in heaven forgive your transgressions."

– Mark 11:22-26 (NASB)

Proclamation #30. The Lord's Prayer.

> *"God's promises are like a bag full of golden coins that God pours out at the feet of His adopted children and says: "Take what you will!"*
>
> – William Spurstowe

"Our Father who is in heaven, Hallowed be Your name. Your kingdom come. Your will be done, On earth as it is in heaven. Give us this day our daily bread. 'And forgive us our debts, as we also have forgiven our debtors. 'And do not lead us into temptation, but deliver us from evil. For Yours is the kingdom and the power and the glory forever. Amen."

– Matthew 6:9-13 (NASB)

Here's my amplified proclamation of The Lord's Prayer. Proclaim this out loud with some gusto. Enjoy and share.

LORD GOD, I declare that you are my father. Yes, the all-powerful and all-knowing Lord of the Universe is my Dad through adoption in Christ Jesus (Gal.4:5). I am his blood-bought redeemed child. I have not received a spirit of slavery leading to fear again, but I have received a spirit of adoption by which I cry out, "Abba! Father!" (– Rom.8:15)

To all evil spirits, large and small, I proclaim my Father, as you well know, is a Heavenly Father, and he sits in the heavens and laughs at you, scoffs at you, and has shattered you with his rod of iron (– Ps.2:1-9). The heavens rule, not evil (– Dan.4:26). My God is far above all rule and authority and power and dominion, and every name that is named, not only in this age but also in the one to come (– Eph.1:21).

I Talk Back to the Devil

Lord, I proclaim the holiness of your name. While others curse your name, use your name in vain, and drag your name through the mud, there is coming a day when at the name of Jesus every knee will bow, of those who are in heaven and on earth and under the earth, and ... every tongue will confess that Jesus Christ is Lord, to the glory of God the Father (– Phil.2:10-11).

Lord God Almighty, my Rock, my Fortress, my Strength, and my Deliverer: I proclaim in my life, with my family, and where your gospel goes throughout the world that your kingdom and your will *will* be done and not what Satan wants to occur. No weapon of hell will prosper against your kingdom cause (– Rom.8:31-39). No man or devil can thwart what you have willed (Rom.9:19, 28) for this earth. I declare your Word which states you want heaven to impact this earth and so it will. Your mission will be successful on earth and the gates of hell will not prevail (– Mt.16:18).

Lord, I thank you for providing me daily bread. My faithful Father supplies all my needs according to his riches in glory (– Phil.4:19). My heavenly Father knows about all of my needs and he will take care of me and uphold me as I seek first his kingdom and his righteousness, and all my needs will be taken care of and I don't have to worry (– Mt.6:33-34).

Heavenly Father, forgive my many sins as I forgive those who have sinned against me. I release them and will not live in bitterness.

Thank you, my Rock and my Redeemer, for keeping me from temptation. Thank you for keeping evil at bay in my life. Thank you for exposing the schemes of the devil arrayed against me. Thank you for the full armor of God that you have given me to extinguish all the flaming arrows of the evil one (– Eph.6:10-18).

God I declare yours is the kingdom and not the devil's. Yours is the power and not Satan's. And yours is the glory forever and not Lucifer's or any man that'll ever walk this planet. In Jesus's name, amen!

I Talk Back to the Devil

About the Author

Doug earned his Bachelor of Fine Arts degree from Texas Tech University and his certificates in both Theological and Biblical Studies from Knox Theological Seminary (Dr. D. James Kennedy, Chancellor). Giles was fortunate to have Dr. R.C. Sproul as an instructor for several classes.

Doug Giles is the host of *The Doug Giles Podcast*, the co-founder and co-host of the *Warriors & Wildmen Podcast* (1M+ downloads) and the man behind ClashDaily. com. In addition to driving ClashDaily.com (300M+ page views), Giles is the author of several #1 Amazon bestsellers. His book *Psalms of War: Prayers That Literally Kick Ass* (2021) spent 26 weeks at #1 on Amazon. In 2018, Giles was permanently banned from his two million followers on Facebook.

Doug is also an artist and a filmmaker, and his online gallery can be seen at DougGiles.Art. His first film, *Biblical Badasses: A Raw Look at*

I Talk Back to the Devil

Christianity and Art, is available via DougGiles. Art.

Doug's writings have appeared in several other print and online news sources, including Townhall.com, The Washington Times, The Daily Caller, Fox Nation, Human Events, USA Today, The Wall Street Journal, The Washington Examiner, American Hunter Magazine, and ABC News.

Currently, Giles pastors Liberty Fellowship in Wimberley, Texas (LibertyTX.org).

Doug and his wife, Margaret, have two daughters, Hannah and Regis. Hannah devastated ACORN with her 2009 nation-shaking undercover videos, and she currently stars in the explosive 2018 Tribeca Documentary, *Acorn and The Firestorm*.

Regis has been featured in *Elle*, *American Hunter*, and *Variety* magazines. Regis is also the author of a powerful new book titled, *Let Go!*

Regis and Hannah are both black belts in Gracie/Valente Jiu-Jitsu.

To check out Doug's art, books, videos, sermons, news portal and cigars go to DougGiles.net. He's on Instagram @TheGilesWay and on X @TheArtOfDoug.

Books by Doug Giles

Lionhearted: Making Young Christian Males Rowdy Biblical Men

John The Baptist: A Rude Awakening Precedes A Great Awakening

The Wildman Devotional: A 50 Day Devotional for Men

Dear Christian: Your Fear Is Full of Crap

Psalms of War: Prayers That Literally Kick Ass

If Masculinity is 'Toxic,' Call Jesus Radioactive

Biblical Badasses: The Women

The Art of Joe: The Political Brilliance of President Biden

Would Jesus Vote For Trump?

Rules For Radical Christians: 10 Biblical Disciplines for Influential Believers

Pussification: The Effeminization Of The American Male

I Talk Back to the Devil

Raising Righteous And Rowdy Girls

Raising Boys Feminists Will Hate

Rise, Kill and Eat: A Theology of Hunting From Genesis to Revelation.

If You're Going Through Hell, Keep Going

My Grandpa is a Patriotic Badass

A Coloring Book for College Cry Babies

Sandy Hook Massacre: When Seconds Count, Police Are Minutes Away

The Bulldog Attitude: Get It or ... Get Left Behind

A Time To Clash

10 Habits of Decidedly Defective People: The Successful Loser's Guide to Life

Political Twerps, Cultural Jerks, Church Quirks

www.ingramcontent.com/pod-product-compliance
Lightning Source LLC
Chambersburg PA
CBHW071706090426
42738CB00009B/1681